P9-EKW-853

Praise for *The Food Lover's Garden*

Remember the last time you stood in the cold cereal aisle
at the grocery store and a little voice said, "There's a better way"?
I know. You've never grown a garden. You're not that comfortable
in the kitchen. What if one little book fixed all that? With
The Food Lover's Garden in hand, there's just no excuse,
no reason to deprive yourself again this summer. Soon,
you'll be eating to your heart and health's content

MARYJANE BUTTERS maryjanesfarm.com

One does not expect a gardening book to make one's
mouth water with anticipation. Jenni Blackmore's second helping,
The Food Lover's Garden, does just that. The crisp photographs,
lushly painted illustrations, and delicious text lead the reader
from the garden to the kitchen and pantry with
anticipation of culinary delight.

DARRELL E. FREY author, *The Bioshelter Market Garden*

As a chef who has, for a good portion of his career, had an
ongoing love affair with food that is prepared close to home by
people who care, *The Food Lover's Garden* resonates with me. It's
earnest yet thoughtful musings on taste, smell, the challenges of
growing food and society's changing respect for those ingredients
gives me hope. I love the recipes … well-thumbed pages
will be the best legacy that this book can leave.

MICHAEL HOWELL Executive Chef,
The Green Turtle Club, Abaco, Bahamas, and Executive
Director, Devour The Food Film Fest, Wolfville, NS

CALGARY PUBLIC LIBRARY

DEC   2017

The Food Lover's Garden will be your "one stop shop"
for everything from seed to plate. For anyone new to home
gardening and looking for a nurturing, personal coach to expertly
navigate you through the how-to's: meet author, Jenni Blackmore.
This book will leave you feeling empowered and ready
to launch your own journey to food self-sufficiency.

LISA KIVIRIST author, *Soil Sisters* and *Homemade for Sale*

If you know a foodie who wants to get up close and personal
with their food — perhaps you? — this is the perfect guide to their
first garden. Jenni gives you the information you need to choose
your list of plants based upon the meals you will eventually
prepare with them. This is a beautiful and practical
addition to every foodie's library.

DEBORAH NIEMANN author, *Homegrown and Handmade*,
Ecothrifty, and *Raising Goats Naturally*

THE
food lover's
GARDEN

THE
food lover's
GARDEN

growing, cooking, and eating well

Jenni Blackmore

new society
PUBLISHERS
www.newsociety.com

Copyright © 2017 by Jenni Blackmore.
All rights reserved.

Cover design by Diane McIntosh
Interior design by Setareh Ashrafologhalai
Cover image credit © iStock
All illustrations by Jenni Blackmore, © 2017

Printed in Canada. First printing March 2017.

Inquiries regarding requests to reprint all or part of *The Food Lover's Garden* should be addressed to New Society Publishers at the address below. To order directly from the publishers, please call toll-free (North America) 1-800-567-6772, or order online at www.newsociety.com

Any other inquiries can be directed by mail to:
New Society Publishers
P.O. Box 189, Gabriola Island, BC V0R 1X0, Canada
(250) 247-9737

LIBRARY AND ARCHIVES CANADA CATALOGUING IN PUBLICATION

Blackmore, Jenni, author
    The food lover's garden : growing, cooking, and eating well /
Jenni Blackmore.

Issued in print and electronic formats.
ISBN 978-0-86571-842-5 (softcover).--ISBN 978-1-55092-637-8 (PDF).--
ISBN 978-1-77142-231-4 (HTML)

    1. Vegetable gardening. 2. Cooking (Vegetables). 3. Vegetables--
Preservation. I. Title.

SB321.B63 2017 635   C2017-900408-5   C2017-900409-3

Funded by the   Financé par le
Government   gouvernement
of Canada   du Canada

New Society Publishers' mission is to publish books that contribute
in fundamental ways to building an ecologically sustainable and just
society, and to do so with the least possible impact on the environment,
in a manner that models this vision.

Dedicated to my family

to my sons, Nikolas, Jason and Martin, who survived my
'kitchen klutz' years intact, along with their (highly exaggerated)
accounts of my more memorable culinary catastrophes; to my wonderful husband Calum who supports me every step of the way and finally
to my parents, Iris and Clifford, who somehow managed to seed my
appreciation of what's fresh and real, way back when in the industrial
North of England. Thank you all from the bottom of my heart.

Contents

In the Kitchen

In the Beginning...

THE IDEA TO WRITE *The Food Lover's Garden* came to me a few years ago. I was developing a community garden and I realized that many young (and not so young) people had little or no experience preparing vegetables from their natural state—that is, taking them from the garden to the plate. As a result, a lot of wonderful food was left to wither and rot. A very sad state of affairs!

As food prices spiral and it becomes more of a challenge to eat healthily and well, the term "home-grown" is reclaiming deeper meanings of empowerment and sustainability. It's my hope that home-grown will soon become a commonly used household expression again and that celebrations at harvest time will echo with the historically joyous significance of growing our own food. For this to happen, knowing what to do with the gaggle of garden goodies is just as important as knowing how to grow them in the first place. That's what this book's about: a how-to on the full meal deal, so to speak.

Necessity is indeed the mother of invention but I don't want the element of need to overshadow the more glorious benefits of eating food we've grown ourselves. For one thing, we can be sure such food has not been laced with any toxic additives at any stage of its production; for another we will be tasting truly fresh, picked when perfectly ripe, food as it's supposed to taste, guaranteed to have more flavor and be infinitely more delicious than anything purchased at a food-mart. Another, often neglected yet equally important benefit of "grass-roots" home food production is that a handful of beans or a handsome butternut squash we've grown ourselves will not only supply high quality nutrition for our bodies, but will also nurture our souls to a degree that has to be experienced to be believed. We are meant to produce at least some of our own food. Of this much I'm certain.

There are so many things in today's society that we don't need and would probably be better off without, but food isn't one of them. It's a basic necessity of life, if not the prime necessity, and yet we have relatively little control over or connection to the food we eat. By now I'm doubtless starting to sound like I have an unhealthy obsession with food, but I don't think so, even though, when I see what so many people are eating and what they're training their children to eat, I'm more than saddened, I'm horrified!

Patterns of poor eating impact in such a negative way on quality of life and the benefits of eating healthily (which are many) are easy to claim. It really is a no-brainer. Poor eating habits and sub-standard nutrition surreptitiously steal the joy out of life. And without a doubt, life is meant to be a very joyous business.

Of course, not everyone has the facilities to grow and store all the vegetables they might need for a year, but most of us will have the opportunity to grow at least some. And then what? Sure, it's great to grow potatoes but if the only potatoes we're familiar with have always been in the form of French-fries it might be challenging to transform our crop into the many, many other taste-tempting dishes potatoes are capable of becoming. The humble potato, so often served as a bland accompaniment to "the main meal," deserves better. In essence this book is a different kind of gourmet travel guide, it traces the journey from the garden to the supper table, starting with a few seeds and ending with a plethora of mouth-watering meals.

▶ These "basil boots" prove that, with a little TLC, plants will grow just about anywhere.

I'm a competent gardener and a passable cook and had initially envisioned *The Food Lover's Garden* as a solitary project. That was before my wonderful friend and chef extraordinaire, Jennifer, began making sunchoke pâté, using the excess sunchoke (also called Jerusalem Artichoke) harvest. It was the first year I'd grown sunchokes and I'd been content to serve them simply steamed or roasted. Big mistake! Sunchoke pâté is absolutely delicious. (You can find this recipe in Chapter Fourteen.) A couple of other friends have also shared their favorite recipes to add to this eclectic selection of fab food, culinary creativity, and green thumb know-how.

The purpose of this book is to turn hesitant gardeners into avid vegetable growers who delight in eating and sharing the delicious produce they've grown. There's a special kind of joy that comes from growing your own food and my desire is to make that joy more widely available.

My plan is to keep things simple, partly by featuring veggies that are superbly (and absurdly) easy to grow, and which are also especially tasty and nutritious. Coming up with the list of what to feature turned out to be quite difficult. There are so many plants that fit those requirements and I didn't want this book to become encyclopaedic. The list of suggested crops is far from comprehensive and concentrates on the plants that produce well and offer lots of scope in the kitchen.

I live and garden on a small windswept island, surrounded by the Atlantic Ocean. The seemingly ever-present onshore winds and summertime temperatures, which are almost always several to many degrees cooler than those inland, create their own set of challenges, and the soil is nothing to brag about either. I mention this now because I expect that most people reading this book will not have been blessed with a gently sloping, southerly facing patch of fluffy rich soil and some might even be thinking, "this would be nice someday, maybe, when..." Stop right there! With a little ingenuity and the right kind of care, gardens can sprout up and flourish in the most unexpected places; in a leaky bucket, for instance or even in an old boot.

There are always challenges, yes, but challenges need not be deterrents and I've come to believe that a challenge can in fact be a good thing. It encourages a full assessment of any given situation and the subsequent design of a plan that will maximize on the available strengths and devise creative solutions for the potential problems. Whether we like it or not, every day is an adventure, some more exciting than others, and I do believe that flexibility is the key to enjoying both the smooth and the bumpy parts of the journey.

Flexibility in the kitchen opens up a whole world of possibilities, allowing personal preferences to give meals an inimitable bonus. Here I find myself smiling as I imagine some worst case scenarios of a chef-gone-wild, from zero to eighty, with no previous experience whatsoever. I had an Aunt a lot like that, someone with oodles of enthusiasm but without the know-how to back it up. Some of her culinary catastrophes were quite epic and I loved her the more for each and every one of them but, not to worry, I learnt a lot from her mistakes and this book will supply recipes, or at least some helpful how-tos!

The recipes which are mine are "easy-peasies" and all feature the selection of vegetables described in the Garden section of this book. Like most people I see time as a precious ingredient. I'm also passionate about healthy eating so it's pretty much a given that the recipes in this book are all simple, affordable, and highly nutritious. Good news is, they're also flexible. It's a wonderful thing to let the garden dictate what's for supper and over time it becomes second nature to substitute and reinvent, based on seasonal availability. Sadly this innate skill has been diluted over recent generations by the artificiality of commercial food supplies. Food processing and delivery systems are also robbing us of proper nutrition and, definitely, taste and texture, while at the same time introducing chemical agents into our bodies and nurturing our complete dependency on unsustainable supply networks that can collapse at any time.

There are many excellent, common-sense reasons for growing our own food but the one that doesn't get mentioned nearly enough comes right from the heart. Yes, very simply, it's love; for one's self, for each other, and for this most beautiful planet.

"I grew this and I cooked it just for you, in my own special way." What could make a meal more special than that?

In the Garden

1

Deep Down 'n Dirty

getting started in the garden

AS WITH MOST noble pursuits, some specific tools are required. In this case, exactly which tools will vary greatly depending on the size of the garden and the condition of the soil. Shopping for gardening tools is a lot like visiting a toy store—wannit, wannit, needit, gotta have … and so on, but Christmas is no doubt already a few months gone, so let's get real.

As with most things, you pretty much get what you pay for but, whereas I'm sure it would be nice to have a top of the line and coincidingly expensive spade, I'm quite happy with my mid-range one, and while I prefer the traditional look and feel of wooden shafts, I have a really bad habit of leaving tools lying around outside for extended periods, which causes the wood to swell, splinter and crack, so fiberglass shafts are definitely my wiser choice. They're also a bit lighter in weight which can make a difference over the long haul.

When I started my garden the tool I used most was a pickax, but only because my circumstances were extreme. I'm pretty certain that most new gardeners (hopefully) won't need a pick, but this tool does help to demonstrate two important points. Firstly, size. Most basic tools come in more than one size. I'm fairly short, with a light frame, so I can control a light-weight pick way more efficiently than the heavy duty clunker my husband favors. It took me a while to figure this out, but my body was very happy when I did. The other thing I learned from my pickaxing days is that needs change over time. I almost never use a pick now, only occasionally to remove a boulder or such.

Lesson here choose tools sized appropriately and expect needs to change. For instance, a couple of levels down from a pick would be a spading fork, probably a more likely and better choice for most situations.

NECESSARY TOOLS

A spading fork is a great all round tool, perfect for breaking into hard packed ground simply by inserting the tines and rocking them back and forth to aerate the soil and allow moisture to penetrate, yet equally useful when that hard pack has been transformed into rich, fluffy soil which has produced a great harvest of, let's say leeks, to gently pry the crop from the soil.

Spades are definitely designed for digging and they come in a variety of styles and sizes. Some have a slightly rounded face, others are totally flat; some have a slightly rounded cutting edge while others have a straight edge, some taper slightly and some have a narrow ledge along the top edge for a foot to press down on. The resulting difference between each design is fairly minimal and really, a spade is a spade. They are useful for cutting through turf and such, but generally I favor a fork over a spade as I find it easier to penetrate the hard stuff and less disruptive in established gardens.

Shovels come in a range of styles similar to spades and in fact the exact designation of which is what gets a bit blurry. Shovel or spade, they're similar but not really interchangeable. The longer, straight handle of a typical shovel interferes with digging in confined areas but facilitates tossing or spreading of soil, compost, etc., over larger areas. If it's a choice between a spade or a shovel a lot will depend on the size of the garden. A modest raised bed or two might be better served by a small spade. It's all relative, and determining factors will also include cost, as well as availability of storage space: the more tools the more space required to store them.

Hoes—once again a myriad of choices here: square or pointy edged, angled or straight, big, small. I think they're mostly designed for hilling up rows, chopping out weeds between the rows and marking drills (shallow indentations for planting seeds in rows). I used to have a triangular shaped hoe which I quite liked but then I fell in love with the three and four pronged fork hoes (sometimes called cultivators) which I use almost exclusively now.

Hand Tools

Trowels—it's definitely worth investing in a couple of good trowels. I have a deeply cupped, heavy duty dude that's great for mixing up a bucket full of soil, while the narrow, smaller trowel makes holes perfect for inserting transplants, and can dig in close without damaging adjacent roots.

Short handled fork hoes are virtually indispensable as they're perfect for loosening soil, for seeding and later for cultivating between plants. It's nice to have a couple of sizes as well as a neat little combo tool called a mattock which is both a claw and a small flat-edged hoe.

Other Essentials

A rubber kneeling mat—so much nicer than kneeling on wet, muddy ground or sharp, pointy rocks.

Well-fitting gardening gloves with rubberized palms and breathable backs—to protect hands from cuts, scrapes, splinters and thorns. The floppy cotton ones are a just plain silly as far as I'm concerned.

Buckets or recycled pails—several of these along with a few empty plant pots and a sizeable heavy gauge plastic carrier basket for green refuse, trimmings and harvesting.

▶ Tools or toys? Playing in the dirt is always fun!

A START-UP TOOL KIT

I definitely favor raised beds and smaller plots and I mulch heavily, so my tool list reflects the requirements of this method of growing food rather than the more traditional method of working one large square of tilled ground.

Thinking in terms of setting up a smallish urban garden, here is a list of equipment that I think would be necessary. This is the bare minimum starter kit and I'm sure there are a few extra tools I'd want to add over time, but I think I could manage with these.

A digging fork and a four pronged fork hoe with fiberglass shafts, both sized to fit me. Two good quality trowels and at least one hand rake. Kneeling pad and gloves, watering can and pails. A sharp knife, scissors, sturdy stakes, twine, an indelible marker and tags to label seeded rows.

I've found it very useful to tie streamers of bright orange flagging tape to the short-handled tools because they easily get misplaced in the greenery, and I always buy my gloves in bulk packs because they have a habit of slithering off to parts unknown.

Yard sales and especially moving sales are great places to pick up gardening tools and as gardening tools never stay shiny and new looking for long, used ones will give you an instant "professional" look!

A watering can—definitely one with a removable rose (the perforated spray end) as these tend to clog easily, and preferably one with measurements up the side, which are a big help when mixing up a special mid-season treat of organic plant food such as fish fertilizer.

There are so many rhythms happening in a garden and while writing this I realize that even tool use has its own sequence. During the soil prep times of early spring and late fall it's the long handled tools that come into play, while the actual seeding and nurturing of plants requires the more intimate closeness that comes with hand tools.

WHAT PLANTS NEED

To flourish, that is, to fulfill their given purpose successfully, all plants have three basic requirements: relatively good soil, water and sunlight, in degrees which vary according to the plant. Plants have personalities. Some plants are quite happy to prove that less is more by doing well with very little of some or all of these requirements, while others are just plain needy, greedy or both, giving the impression that indeed, they can't get enough of a good thing.

Despite these variations there are some generalities that can be applied to the requirements of plants. Let's start with soil. One of the keys to successful gardening depends on how we relate to our soil. Soil is definitely not an inert substance but rather a multifaceted living community which is home to a microcosm of other living organisms, all of which are linked by a frenetically active food chain. Soil science is a far ranging topic and truly fascinating, even for a totally non-scientific intellect such as mine, but here is definitely not the place to begin such a discussion. There are, however, a few key points that need to be mentioned so that the relationship between plants and the stuff they grow in can be better appreciated.

The often used term "soil amendments" simply refers to anything that is added to improve the quality (and therefore the efficiency) of the soil. These amendments fall into two general categories: additives that will improve the texture of the soil and additives that will improve its chemical profile. In terms of the human body these could be loosely represented by fibre, proteins and vitamins.

WHAT SOIL NEEDS

There are many types of soil, ranging from sandy to hard packed clay, which all consist of varying amounts of organic matter, silt, grit and stone. Bulk is important in sandy soil because it helps to prevent erosion and loss of nutrients through leaching. Bulk (think fiber) also helps to make clay soil more friable (fluffier) and it creates spaces where oxygen and moisture can penetrate.

Mulch, initially, is a layer of organic material applied to the surface of the soil to supress weed growth and help maintain moisture in the summer months, and to protect the soil from packing and leaching during the winter. Over time, good organic mulch, such as seaweed, leaves, grass clippings and straw will provide bulk and will also release a host of nutrients as it rots down.

Nutrients are grouped into Macro and Micro categories. Often, macronutrients are given more consideration than micronutrients because they are required in larger amounts to support healthy growth, but in fact micronutrients have an equally important role to play. There are some quirky home remedies and seemingly extreme claims for success that are based on additives from the kitchen and the medicine cabinet, such as antacid tablets, Epsom salts and banana skins. Weird as they might seem these claims are usually based on solid science—antacid tablets for calcium, Epsom salts for magnesium and banana skins for potassium and phosphorous.

The pH balance of the soil is also important to food production. Most vegetables tend to prefer a pH of around seven or slightly less. Soil that is too alkaline (over seven) can restrict nutrient absorption and result in sickly plants. Acidic soil is sometimes referred to as being "sour", whereas alkaline soil will be called "sweet". The pH level can usually be adjusted with the addition of some pelletized lime or wood ash to sweeten, coffee grounds to promote acidity. Simple test kits are available at garden centres which will determine

MACRO AND MICRO NUTRIENTS

Just a little basic info on soil science as it relates to plants. It's fairly common knowledge that plants need Nitrogen (N), Phosphorous (P), Potassium (K) and Carbon (C). On typical fertilizer labels the first three are listed as three numbers such as 20-20-20, or 20-5-5 (which has four times more Nitrogen than Phosphorous and Potassium). I would highly recommend never, ever using chemical fertilizers. They are damaging to both our health and our soil.

Trace elements, which occur in minute amounts are far less familiar but equally important. They need to be in a subtle but crucial balance and it's really much better not to mess with trace elements. They can be added as rock phosphate, green sand or granite dust if absolutely necessary. Some of the lesser macronutrients and micronutrients are Boron (B), Calcium (Ca), Copper (Cu), Iron (Fe), Magnesium (Mg), Manganese (Mn), Molybdenum (Mo), Selenium (Se), Silicon (Si), Sulphur (S) and Zinc (Zn).

Hopefully the list alone will clarify why it's much better to rely on kelp meal and fish fertilizers, manures, organic mulches and compost for the plants' nutritional needs.

▲ A three box composting system— kitchen waste in one end, fluffy rich growing medium out the other.

whether this is necessary. Testing the pH level is not an essential procedure but it never hurts to do a little trouble shooting prior to planting in order to avoid potential disappointment.

Compost is the truly magical ingredient that plays a huge role in the development of healthy plants and vigorous plant growth. Compost is made by piling organic food waste and plant material and encouraging aerobic (that is aerated) decomposition. Compost encourages an infinite number of microscopic nematodes and protozoa to proliferate in the soil and become part of a complex food web that consists of worms, beetles and a host of other insects, bacteria and fungi, who all do their part in breaking down the cellulose fibres in organic bulk and transforming them into sugars that can be taken up by the delicate root hairs of the plants.

That's a very simple explanation of the relationship between plants and their growing medium but hopefully it's enough to stress the fact that an adequate food source for plants depends on a number of factors and not solely on the pre-existing nature of the soil. The pre-existing soil in my garden was pretty much solid clay topped with a scant layer of humus. It was highly acidic and not in the least hospitable to most plants. The soil I grow in now has been "transformed" over several years by the addition of much organic bulk, a variety of manures, and compost, into a fertile oasis that produces abundant crops of the most delicious vegetables. It definitely can be done with just a little effort and a bit of know-how!

CREATING GARDEN BEDS

There are several ways to construct a garden bed. A generation ago the most common way was to till or dig up whatever ground was available and sprinkle in some chemical fertilizer. Yikes! Fortunately chemical fertilizers are being recognized for what they are: a threat to our health and the health of our soil, and digging is being replaced by more efficient techniques.

The two methods I favor are raised bed and lasagna gardens. They are actually somewhat similar and equally simple to construct.

Raised Bed Gardens are built up on top of the existing ground, usually using a wooden frame. The frame is then filled with a fertile mix of soil, compost and manure. Raised beds can be any shape but are usually square or oblong depending on the space you have to work with. The important thing to remember about raised beds is that they're never trodden on. Because the soil is never compressed it remains light and fluffy. Oblong beds are not more than four feet wide to allow an easy access to the centre of the bed from either side. Eight inches or deeper is an optimum depth for soil in a raised bed.

The Lasagna Bed is another popular and highly efficient method of creating a growing place. The lasagna bed is quite similar to a raised bed in that the growing area is created on top of the existing ground level and, therefore, does not require any strenuous digging.

Lasagna beds are well named as they're composed of layers, much like the similarly named pasta dish. In this case the layers consist of organic materials such as grass clippings, leaves, seaweed, spoiled straw, manure and compost interspersed with occasional layers of soil. Note: two thin layers of an ingredient are much more effective than one thicker layer.

Each of these layers or ingredients adds its own particular set of nutrients to the mix and I'm sure that all the insects and microbes go crazy trying to decide where they like to hang out the most. It's their activity that will blend the layers into amazingly fertile soil.

COMPOST

Just about anything organic can be composted, within reason of course. The process is simple enough: food waste, grass clippings, manure, leaves, etc., are layered, perhaps with a little soil and forest duff, in a pile, usually enclosed with wire mesh or wooden slats. When a sizeable amount has been collected the pile is turned regularly to aerate it. This important step prevents the compost pile from turning into a slimy, smelling mess by causing the ingredients to breakdown anaerobically, that is, without air. Simple guidelines for managing compost: if it smells—it's too wet, if it has ants living in it—it's too dry.

▲ Raised beds in winter.

▲ Raised beds in early spring.

▲ Raised beds in early summer.

▲ Spring greens growing in an old tractor tire.

First off, cover the chosen plot with newspaper and then cardboard. A couple of layers is better than one, if supply permits. This really important first step ensures that no pernicious weeds (weeds with root systems designed to take over the planet) can force their way up into the garden. Mulching with cardboard might seem weird but this is a simple yet effective way to deter already well-established weeds from reappearing. It also holds water well and over time will break down providing more organic matter.

The ingredients of a lasagna bed can be roughly grouped as green (grass clippings, kitchen waste and other fresh plant material) or brown (straw, dead leaves and soil) and it's a good idea to alternate between green and brown layers as much as possible. A little compost goes a long way by importing trillions of hard working bacteria and more than a few worms, and certainly more than one layer of compost will push the decomposition process into overdrive. Fresh manure, which is referred to as being "hot," will also speed up the process by heating everything up, but it should only be placed in the lower layers of the bed so that the delicate roots of plants will not reach it and get "burned." (Normally manure should be aged for at least a year before it's applied to the soil.)

The top layer of the bed will be soil which is then covered with straw or dry leaves to prevent any weed seeds sprouting on the surface. Ideally a lasagna bed should be set up in the fall so it has the winter to meld into a rich, fluffy growing medium but shallow rooted plants can thrive in a newly established lasagna bed, especially if the top layer of soil is fairly thick (a minimum 2 inches) and the bed is kept well-watered.

The area chosen for any garden bed should have full sun all day or at least as close to that as possible. It should not be heavily shadowed by large trees because while the branches are stealing light, the roots of the trees will be gobbling up nutrients intended for the veggies. Dense shrubbery and small trees reasonably close by are not such a problem and in fact might provide a welcomed wind break.

Both of these methods of creating garden beds produce very fertile soil which can be densely planted, because there's plenty of plant food to go around. So, even if the area you have to work with initially might seem to be insufficient, don't be discouraged. You will be amazed at how much food even a large pot or a well-tended window box can produce. But be warned, growing food is addictive! You may be starting with a two foot by four foot box on a sunny balcony, but keep in mind how the journey of a thousand miles begins. :)

Now that the nitty-gritty dirt building stuff has been dealt with it's time to plant—well, at least to consider what to plant. Drum roll please, as I present the list of suggestions: all versatile, tasty and super easy to grow vegetables with a sprinkle of herbs and flowers thrown in for a little extra pizzazz. I have grouped the vegetables, two to a chapter, and have listed them accordingly.

▶ Nasturtiums blooming
happily in poor soil by the
path to the feed shed.

WHAT TO GROW

Potatoes and Leeks	Squash and Garlic
Beets and Greens	Beans and Onions
(summer and winter)	Tomatoes and Cucumbers

Selected Herbs

Chives	Dill
Parsley	Mint
Summer Savory	Cilantro / Coriander

Perennials (they come up year after year)

Rhubarb	Blackcurrants
Egyptian Onions	Chamomile
Sunchokes	

Just a Couple of Edible Flowers

Nasturtiums

Poppies—for their seeds.

NB only two species of poppy seeds are edible (when cooked): *papaver somniferum* and *papaver paeoniflorum*, so it's important to know exactly what type of poppy you're planting.

Some of the edibles on the list might not be your super favorites, and some you might even think you don't like one bit, but trust me, such preconceived notions might need revising come harvest time, with all those fresh picked flavors coming straight from your very own garden.

2

Potatoes & Leeks

CONSIDER THE PLIGHT of the humble potato! Perhaps the most under-appreciated, yet surely the most accommodating vegetable of all, best known chipped and deep fried into the main stay of fast food outlets the world over. Other supporting roles have it peeled, boiled and mashed; sliced, diced, saturated with mayo and served as the ubiquitous summer stand-by, potato salad; or baked, or roasted—but always in a supporting role. Already quite a few options, but in my opinion none that hold a candle to potato and leek soup, scalloped potatoes (with cheese and onion of course) or potato pie, cheese gnocchi, potato pancakes... I could go on but I'm sure I've made my point.

HOW TO GROW A POTATO

There are many, many varieties of potatoes, each with its own claim to fame: early, late; yellow, purple; roasters, fingerlings... but I'm keeping things simple and just calling a potato a potato for the purposes of this book.

Potatoes are so very easy to grow and they don't need much soil to grow in. I'm sure I'm not the only one who's found a couple of long forgotten spuds in the back of a cupboard, with their tangled white shoots looking like alien tendrils preparing to break out and snatch the family pet. These sprouted potatoes can be planted and they

▲ It's always a good idea to plant several types of potatoes. Each type will bring its own particular attributes to the kitchen.

might well produce a few small potatoes. However, it's much better to buy some seed potatoes at a garden centre or farm supply store.

You won't need many. Each "eye" of a potato will produce its own mother plant, so one potato can be cut into several pieces, with care taken to ensure that each piece has at least one eye. It doesn't hurt to let the cut skin dry out for a day or so. This is not essential but certainly helps to prevent rot and fungal attack. The potato plant is a vine and it can be encouraged to grow upwards rather than sprawl outwards. Vertical growth means a smaller footprint which in turn means more room for other plants. This is especially useful when space is limited.

Small Space Planting

To encourage vertical growth, potatoes are planted in an enclosed but open ended (top and bottom) structure. This can be as simple as a vertical cylinder of snow fencing, a barrel or a specially constructed box. Whatever the structure, it is not filled to the top with soil. A few inches at the base are all that is required to cover the cut up pieces of seed potato. Once the shoots appear above the surface of the soil they are surrounded with an organic mulch, usually straw or leaves and this process is repeated several times, thereby encouraging the vine, along with its fruit, to keep reaching upwards instead of sideways. This stacking technique will save a lot of space as the potatoes can be planted much closer together. However, this method only works well with strains that are of an indeterminate variety, that is, which grow on a vine that does not have a predetermined length. Most of the more common varieties of potato are determinate and will only produce one largish clump of potatoes. Only a few late season varieties will keep producing. Having said this it's important to note that all potatoes like to be mulched at least once, as they tend to grow very close to the surface. Mulching prevents some of the crop from becoming "sunburnt"—read: green and toxic.

Regular Spacing

If space is not an issue and the seed potatoes are being planted the traditional in-ground way, each plant will require about 18 inches of elbow room to flourish. They will definitely produce better if they are mulched at least once. Along the shore where I live it was common practice, not so long ago, to grow a winter's worth of potatoes in banks of eel grass (a dark colored sea grass that washes up every fall and that looks a lot like shredded paper). That practice is a good indicator of how little actual soil potatoes require. However, they prefer their soil to be slightly acidic. No lime is needed here as alkaline soil might encourage the growth of scab.

When to Plant

Potatoes are super easy to grow in that, once planted, they can be forgotten about, pretty much, until it's time to dig them up. Probably the most crucial factor for success is timing. In those first heady days of warm spring sunshine, when my green thumb is itching and I'm thinking it's probably time to plant potatoes, I've learned (the hard way) to wait a couple of weeks at least. Potatoes really do not like cold soil and it takes more than a couple of balmy days to warm the soil enough to suit potatoes. Even if they don't simply rot and turn into nasty smelling slime, they'll probably go into a non-productive sulk if the temperature of the soil is not to their liking. There's nothing to be gained by planting too early.

It's useful to remember that soil which may feel warm enough on top will be several degrees colder a couple of inches below the surface. A hand laid on the surface of the soil will tell a different story to a finger poked deep into the soil. It's not unusual to discover ice crystals six to eight inches below the surface well into May, at least around here, and they don't do a thing for warming up the soil!

Once established, each potato eye will produce a leafy plant which is a couple of feet high and similar in breadth. The plants produce pretty purple, blue, pink or white flowers with yellow centers. These will begin to die off after a week or so and eventually the plant itself will begin to wither and turn brown. By that time the days will be considerably shorter and cooler and a sense of fall will be creeping into the air.

When to Harvest

It's best to harvest potatoes a couple of weeks before the first frost, leaving enough time to allow them to "cure" for a couple of days in the sun. It's important not to leave potatoes exposed to daylight for long as this will cause them to turn green and poisonous. A short, gentle sun-bake will toughen up the skin a bit so the crop can be stored more successfully. After a day or so the excess soil will have

▲ Harvesting potatoes is always more fun with a helper.

dried and can be easily brushed off before the potatoes are layered in wood chips, or between sheets of newsprint in open weave containers such as plastic laundry baskets, and stored in a cool dark place. Again, potatoes should not be exposed to light for too long as they will turn green and become toxic due to a concentration of solanine, which is the potato's natural defense against pests and fungus.

Harvesting potatoes on a warm fall day is a truly special experience, somewhat reminiscent of a treasure hunt, with potatoes tumbling out of the ground in exuberant excess. This is definitely an experience worth sharing and certainly enough to counter the weary reasoning against growing potatoes, which always revolves around the low cost and excess availability of potatoes in supermarkets.

This reasoning doesn't touch on the alarming number of times commercially produced potatoes are sprayed (there is even a spray to kill the blossoms) in order to accelerate their growth and the fact that a potato is like a sponge, absorbing whatever is in the soil around it. I prefer just a little salt on my potatoes, thank you. And besides that, the pleasure of the "treasure hunt," with some extra little hands along to "help," does not have a price.

LEEKS

I've chosen leeks to keep potatoes company in this chapter, primarily because leek and potato soup is perhaps my all-time favorite soup. They do share other commonalities, the prime one being that they are both harvested at approximately the same time. Also, each plant produces a single, mid to late season crop, and by that I mean when a potato plant is dug up for harvesting, that's it for that plant and similarly for leeks, whereas a bean plant will keep producing beans and can be harvested (intermittently) for several weeks throughout the summer.

Starting Leeks

Leeks are hardy, but slow to grow, so they don't provide a huge "Wow!" factor for the impatient gardener (and aren't we all?). Leek seeds are about the size of a small, round pin head. I really don't advise planting the seeds directly in the ground for two reasons. For one, the seed is so tiny that it's difficult, if not impossible, to space out evenly and not end up with great clumps that must then be thinned. Boring! And hard on the back. Also, when leeks germinate and the tiny shoots first poke out of the ground they look like delicate blades of grass and continue to look like that for the first couple of months. Consequently there's a huge probability that they will be overshadowed by, and pulled up with, the exuberant array of young weeds that will also be making their debut in those first wonderful days of spring. Leek seeds planted directly in the ground will germinate, no question, but will they flourish?

▲ This tangle of young leeks, originally seeded in a pot, are quite happy to be gently separated and replanted in the ground.

▶ Given a bit of "elbow room" and some rich soil, the delicate leek shoots develop into sturdy, frost tolerant plants.

Growing Leeks

There's also the time element to be considered. They're so slow growing that they need a lot of time, (think 120 days at least to maturity) and certainly, in areas where the frost is late to leave, they probably won't get enough to fulfill their full potential, when planted directly outside. They definitely need to be started inside or purchased from a garden center as seedlings.

Wow! That's enough "cons" to dissuade anyone from growing leeks, but now for the pros. Leeks are very, very hardy. They can be left in the garden, preferably mulched with a heavy winter blankie of straw, through many, many frosts and therefore can be dug, as needed, until the deep winter when the earth turns to stone. Once dug, they will store perfectly, with their roots left with whatever soil that is clinging on, for several more months, in a cold place such as a basement or crawlspace.

Harvesting Leeks

Leeks are highly nutritious and very versatile in the kitchen; they can be added to soups, stews, stir-fries and quiches and can replace onions in just about anything. Leeks, as members of the Allium genus are actually closely related to onions and garlic. If onions are less pungent than garlic, then leeks, with their more subtle and delicate flavor, would place at a similar distance away from onions on a linear scale.

Much like potatoes, leeks are a vegetable that, once in the ground, can be pretty much forgotten about until late summer/early fall when it's time to start harvesting them. Unlike potatoes, which are pretty much harvested all at once before the frost hits, leeks, as mentioned, can be left in the ground and harvested as needed until the ground begins to solidify and a pickax might seem more useful than a shovel.

If a leek is left in the ground over winter it will appear to wither away but the following year it will magically reconstitute itself and produce a magnificent flower head about the size of a tennis ball. Left to open, this mysterious globe will blossom into a myriad of tiny

flowerets which, when they mature and with the help of small flies and other pollinators, will produce enough seeds to plant more leeks than you might ever need in the years to come. I don't plan to focus on seed saving in this book but it is one of my passions and I have to say that as well as being so simple, it's highly satisfying, interesting and economical, and I believe it is a necessary step towards securing our food supply and our ability to prosper sustainably.

all praise the humble potato

Place seeds gently in each shallow drill, sprinkle lettuce just light enough to cover,
not too deep, not too close... but sparse is what it all seems now,
too distant, too forlorn on this grey day of soggy boot-stick earth... and yet,
soon enough the seedlings, sprouted, nudge and jostle,
vie for space within the rows transformed,
a cramped metropolis of leaf and bud, alive with slugs and bugs voracious.
Lay hair-thin leeks in trenches primed rich with humus and dreams of distant soup,
pot shared by white earth-apples already creeping their first fingers
from the wizened skin of kin, snugged warm under an eelgrass quilt,
which will in time reveal a bounty, harvested with no complaints
in this less fertile corner of the plot where tomatoes stubbornly refuse,
zucchinis dither and onions sulk in limbo.
But where potatoes, never loved or lauded half as much as they deserve,
silent and in secret, prodigiously produce.

(Previously published in *Open Heart Farming*)

3

Beets & Greens

I THINK I'D HAVE to include beets on my list of favorite vegetables if only because of their color-magenta at its lushest! When we're choosing food, taste and texture are probably the foremost criteria, with nutritional values a close second, but surely color counts too. Certainly for me it does. There's something distinctly unappetizing about a monochromatic plate of food such as steamed cauliflower, mashed potatoes and baked haddock, for instance. It might not taste bland but it sure looks it, and the first message our brains receive is—*boring*! Definitely in need of a parsley garnish and a couple of lemon wedges, at the very least. A sprinkle of cheddar would help spark up the cauliflower but crispy green beans with a dash of chopped red pepper would be a better choice of vegetable in a predominantly colorless meal.

It's easy enough to transform dull into scintillating with the addition of a little color and a meal is sure to taste better if our other senses have been favorably predisposed. Food shouldn't please only the tongue; our other senses like to be wowed as well.

So, that was my rather (better make that *very*) wordy way of saying that color is a consideration when growing food. Strangely enough there are strains of beets that don't have much color; some that are more pink than purple, one that is yellow and one that is actually white. Yellow beets I can accept because their color, which is dictated by a pigment called betalain, indicates a valid nutritional option, but white beets…?

BEETS

Beets also come in different shapes and this can be useful. The torpedo shaped variety can be easily sliced and might be considered preferable for pickling, while others form relatively small and uniformly round "baby" beets, good for pickling but also good for eating whole. Some are noted for keeping their green tops lush and appealing throughout the growing season (important for anyone who really enjoys steamed beet greens) and yet others have deep red leaves that are almost as sensuous in color as their roots. And then you have the old reliables such as Detroit Dark Red that will grow as big as their space allows (up to small grapefruit size in rich soil), will tolerate a couple of early frosts and will keep in a cool, damp place for several weeks after harvesting, with no special attention. For the record, these are what I usually plant, even though the leaves look pretty raggedy and sad by the end of season.

With beets, as with most crops, the choice of exactly which variety to plant is quite subjective, but safe to say that usually (though not always) the old standbys will perform better than the newer, "designer" strains. Locally sourced seed is much more likely to be acclimatized to local growing conditions and seed saved from one's own home garden is likely the best (and definitely the most affordable) of all. However, beets are biennials, which means they don't produce seed until their second year. While it is possible to get biennials to go to seed, in cold climates it usually requires digging them up to protect them from freezing, keeping them alive throughout the winter, and then replanting in the spring. Then, with a bit of luck, the plant will produce seed during this second season of growth.

▲ Beets—two gifts in one! Both the greens and the roots are delicious.

Planting Beets

Beets are highly nutritious. They are especially noted for their antioxidant, anti-inflammatory and detoxifying attributes, and also as a

very good source of numerous essential minerals. And they're really easy to grow. The seeds look a bit like small, shriveled up peas and are best planted directly into the ground. Each of these seeds is in fact several tiny seeds bundled together so they will tend to sprout in tufts rather than as single shoots, no matter how carefully the seeds are spaced. It's good to soak the seeds for at least a day before planting to help jump-start the germination process—it's not essential but is definitely beneficial. Early spring planting is recommended, with a succession of seedings spaced a couple of weeks apart through April/May. This will supply a more consistent harvest of early greens and baby beets. They like the cool weather so it's best to plant in the early spring, a couple of weeks before the last frost is anticipated but when the soil has warmed to above 50°F (10°C). Beets like having a generous supply of phosphorous so adding a little bone meal (phosphorus) to the soil might well have much the same effect on the beets as a couple of pieces of dark chocolate have on me. :)

Harvesting Beets

Beets aren't usually grown primarily for their greens but the leafy tops, often with tiny beets attached, are quite a treat, especially earlier in the season when they're pulled to thin out the rows, allowing the remaining plants more elbow room. (When pulling young beets, take care not to disturb their neighbors by gently pushing down or otherwise protecting them with one hand while the other hand pulls up.) This process of thinning can continue through the growing season as the beets swell. The green tops tend to toughen up but the roots are delicious simply steamed, baked or grated in a slaw. It's good to keep in mind that beets, as with most vegetables, do lose some of their nutritional value with extended cooking. Less than fifteen minutes steaming, sixty minutes roasting is considered optimal and of course raw is best of all.

Pickled beets are my special favorite and pickling beets is very, very easy: cook beets, slice or cube, pack in jars, cover with spicy vinegar and process. Okay, so maybe not quite that simple. (There are a

◀ Regular harvesting of young beets leaves space for the remaining beets to swell.

few sterilization requirements that can be reviewed in Chapter 15.) The important thing to remember about cooking beets is to keep the skin on. This prevents them from "bleeding out" and losing some of their color and nutrients. Once cooked, the skins will slide off easily and then the beets can be cubed or sliced.

One of my favorite salads consists of ever so lightly sweated spinach, with beets, either pickled or marinated in an oil/balsamic/ maple dressing, topped with goat or feta cheese and, on a perfect day, some toasted walnuts. The taste is amazing and in the context of this text it also works as the perfect segue into growing spinach and many other greens.

GREENS

"Greens" is a catch-all description of a huge and wonderfully diverse range of plants that really do deserve a whole chapter (if not a whole book) to themselves, but as they're going to be sharing this section with beets I'm going to group them very loosely into two main categories (summer greens and hardy greens) and talk about them in fairly broad generalizations, starting with hardy or "shoulder season" greens. Shoulder season greens prefer the cooler temperatures of early spring and late fall and will, in fact, tolerate a fair bit of frost when protected with row cover, clear plastic, recycled windows or just about anything else that will allow light to filter in while keeping the frost from lying on the leaves.

Hardy or "Shoulder Season" Greens

Kale, chard and spinach are common shoulder season greens that can be planted very early in the spring and again in late summer for a late fall/early winter crop that will last right up until the hard freeze. There are several other, perhaps slightly less well known leafy greens such as mustard, mizuna, arugula, pak choi, and mâche (a.k.a. corn salad) that are equally hardy and serve as perfect replacements for the summer salad mixes, which will have gone to seed or wimped out by the first frost.

▲ This fairly narrow bed of spring greens skirting a gravel pathway supplied countless salads for a couple of months.

One of the nice things about growing shoulder season crops (crops that grow in the cooler, shorter days of spring and fall) is that many of the typical pests have not yet arrived or are no longer around. The downside of growing in the shoulder seasons is that everything grows much slower during the shorter hours of daylight, especially in the fall when the window of opportunity contracts with every day, unlike the spring when each day is slightly longer. It does require fairly careful timing to get the seeds sprouted and well established before November/December. Planting seeds eight to twelve weeks before the first frost is the time frame to aim for, which roughly translates as late August/September in temperate zones.

Kale

All the hardy greens are very tasty and nutritious. Perhaps my all-time favorite is kale which I enjoy best eaten raw in a salad. Kale leaves can get a bit tough and strong-tasting as they mature but massaging them gently with olive oil eliminates both of these problems. Oil massages might sound like a time consuming and excessive practice (it certainly did to me when I first heard of it) but actually it's not at all. It can be done as the kale is being torn into pieces; the oil automatically gets "massaged" into the leaves and a couple of extra "scrunches" with both hands completes the job, no problem. And it doesn't take much oil; two or three tablespoons of olive oil for a very large bowl of kale is enough. I always make kale salad in a very large bowl because it tastes so good. A small bowl just doesn't contain enough second helpings. I prefer a sweet dressing, so I usually include maple syrup with lemon juice or balsamic vinegar and either sour cream or mayo. It's worth comparing the caloric and fat counts of mayo and light sour cream. The sour cream appears to be way healthier and it makes a yummy dressing (especially on the spinach/beet salad mentioned earlier).

If I could only pick, or only had room for, one winter green in my garden, it would be kale. For one thing, it's so versatile! It can be... I was going to start this sentence as shown but then it occurred to me that there are lots of things that *can be* done that really would be better left undone so instead of saying kale *can be* I'm saying kale *is* great added to soups and stews, used in typical pesto and dip recipes, ever so lightly steamed, sweated or eaten raw. It will provide an extra power boost to smoothies and, lightly oiled and salted, it can even be baked into "chips."

Kale is said to be one of the most nutritionally dense foods on the planet. It's loaded with vitamin C and K along with other vitamins and a host of minerals including calcium, potassium and magnesium. It has cancer preventing and cholesterol lowering properties along with forty-five different flavonoids that work as anti-inflammatory and anti-oxidizing agents and also help support detoxification. The more I think about kale the more it wows me. Definitely my best fave pick! And certainly, if space is limited, I would say grow kale!

Pak Choi

The other hardy greens I mentioned, pak choi, mizuna, chard and mâche all deserve a place in the shoulder season garden, if there's room, pak choi being my first pick of these. Much like kale it contains powerful antioxidants and phytonutrients that protect cells and reduce inflammation. It's a brilliant source of vitamins C and K and one cup of pak choi contains the same amount of calcium as 125 ml of milk, all for nine calories! As if that were not enough 100 grams provides 149% of daily required vitamin A.

Pak choi? Bok choi? Chinese cabbage? There seems to be a certain amount of confusion regarding the common name for this plant. This confusion can be traced right back to Chinese sources, as the Mandarin name differs from the Cantonese name, which differs from the Wu name, in addition to the fact that many, many different strains have been developed over the centuries it has been cultivated in Asia. Some of the more common strains readily available in North America include a deep burgundy-red leafed variety and one with a very pleasing green (as opposed to white) leaf stalk. For my purposes pak choi or bok choi is the broad veined, low growing hardy green with spoon-shaped leaves (hence sometimes called "soup spoon greens," which is the literal translation of *tatsoi*) that is loaded with nutrition and crazy low on calories.

One thing to keep in mind when growing pak choi: it is susceptible to flea beetles. These minute pests jump from leaf to leaf much like fleas and bite tiny holes, not much bigger than the head of a pin, in the leaves. It's best to cover the seedlings with floating row cover to hopefully prevent this damage.

Mâche

I mention mâche because it is extremely hardy and really does have a sweet and nutty flavor as described in the catalogs, but be warned,

it's very slow to germinate and to grow. It's also a smallish plant that grows quite close to the ground and once cut, when it's about six to eight inches in diameter, that's it. In a nut shell, delicious flavor and texture in salads, but a long wait for a smallish harvest. If space is limited, perhaps not the best choice. Also, if the soil is too warm at seeding time the seed goes dormant. Definitely worth a mention because of its cold tolerance and taste but this wouldn't be my first (or second) choice. Mâche is also known as "corn salad" because it was often found growing wild in grain fields but the name I like best, which is of German origin, is "rapunzel" which is believed to have been the inspiration for the Grimm brother's fairy tale of the same name.

Mizuna

Mizuna, an easy to grow and quite hardy salad green with a slightly peppery taste, is way more accommodating than mâche in that it germinates and grows quickly, producing an on-going harvest which is great. However, the leaf itself is somewhat insubstantial in that there often seems to be more stem than actual leaf, so I find it best to mix with other greens. Having said that, it's often there peeking its jagged-edged leaves out of the ground when not much else is, a fact that seems to miraculously improve upon its texture and flavor, making it a most welcome addition to any cold weather meal.

Swiss Chard

Swiss chard is another green that also seems more welcome under similar circumstances (that is, when there's not much else to choose from) but these mixed feelings are purely subjective—it's just not one of my favorite greens. Many people love chard and it definitely deserves a place in the garden and on the table. It certainly wouldn't be fair not to give it adequate praise. It's most accommodating, in fact even as I write there's a sizeable clump in the garden peeking up out of a foot of snow, and it will doubtless be on the menu sometime soon.

What I think of as "traditional chard" has a broad, white rib running up the center of its leaves, which grow in clumps that can be twelve to eighteen inches high, although smaller, more tender leaves are a better pick. Rainbow chard provides a mix of colored stems, including red and white candy striped, bright orange and yellow. As well as being more visually appealing I find the leaves to be more tender and more delicate in taste, although perhaps the plant itself is not quite as hardy as the older strains. There is also a variety called "rhubarb chard" which, not surprisingly, is red-veined and very pretty and perhaps a tad more resilient than the rainbow strains, but only the white stemmed chard does well in cold conditions.

As with kale, chard offers a host of beneficial nutrients that provide antioxidant, anti-inflammatory and detoxification support along with a flavonoid called Syringic acid which is thought to be useful in controlling blood sugar levels. On the downside, however, chard also has relatively high concentrations of oxalic acid, but then so do spinach, beets, rhubarb and several other common vegetables. One of the negative attributes of oxalic acid is that it can contribute to the formation of kidney stones, but boiling for at least three minutes is thought to reduce these levels.

▲ Summer salad greens—simply beautiful and oh, so delicious!

Summer Greens

It's feels natural to keep dwelling on the cold weather greens, especially when the garden is covered with a glistening white blanket, but it's time to move on to warmer weather thoughts. "Yes! Yes!" shouts my summer-loving inner child. Most of the greens previously mentioned in this chapter are not happy in the heat of July and August and some, though not the biennials, will bolt and produce seed. This is their way of cashing in their chips and leaving it to their progeny to go forth and prosper. Even the greens traditionally thought of as summer loving (I'm going to call them all "lettuce" from now on, even though technically that's not altogether correct) don't like the extreme temperatures usually attributed to July and August and

▲ My favorite ever 25-cent lettuce.

they also will bolt and attempt to produce seed. It's very disheartening to see a favored patch of salad makings turn "stubborn" because, indeed, once lettuce decides to bolt there's not much that can be done to dissuade it.

Preventative measures can include a heavy mulch to keep the roots as cool as possible and regular watering but this also has the negative effect of attracting slugs who will love the cooler, moist space under the mulch, especially as it has a salad bar close by. I have found it best simply to enjoy, and enjoy, and enjoy, and to share, share, share, for just as long as I can, and look for alternatives when the lettuce shows signs of bolting. The first sign is a thickening of the central stem, which will then grow upwards to ensure that the flowers, when they come, will be easily spotted by pollinators. The leaves sprouting out of this stem will appear to become slightly more robust in texture and will develop a bitter taste. Finally, clusters of innocuous flowerets will appear.

Varieties

It's easy to make the mistake of planting too much lettuce, especially as, like most vegetables, it tends to look sparse when the delicate first leaves poke out from the soil. There is also such a plethora of choices to contend with. Decisions, decisions! Who knew there could be so many varieties, all of which exude mega sensory appeal to palates starved of fresh-picked garden greens, and spark a bliss-krieg of wonderful warm weather dreams that tag along keep them company, simply by association?

Seed catalogs can be a very mixed blessing when it comes to deciding which strains to grow because of course every plant shown looks so vibrantly delicious you can almost taste it. But just like chocolate, it's not a good idea to sample them all at one time! Loosely categorized, there's head lettuce, leaf lettuce and salad mixes. Head lettuce, such as iceberg and romaine, tend to form tightly bound heads suited to a single harvest, whereas leaf lettuce lends itself to continual harvesting; that is, picking off the outer leaves at regular, on-going intervals. I tend to prefer the leaf varieties because I feel I can extend the harvest over a longer period of time.

My all-time favorite lettuce is an amazing little guy I paid twenty-five cents for while trolling around an end of season nursery sale. He had infiltrated their regular lettuce packs and had been weeded out and stuck in a pot. Undeterred, he flourished but remained unidentified. His serrated leaves are green, shaded around the edges with a delicate blush of pink. He's the first to come up and the last to bolt, and his growing propensity seems limitless. I can harvest countless wonderfully crisp salads off one single plant and as if this were not enough, he re-seeds himself every year, popping up at various spots around the garden to thrive for yet another season. Without a doubt the best twenty-five cents I ever spent!

Salad Mixes

Over the past few years I've noticed that "salad mixes" have become a regular commercial seed offering. I'm not a great fan of these because all greens are not created equal. Put another way, some plants, just like some kids, don't necessarily play well together. Mustard and mizuna immediately come to mind and I can, in fact, trace my mizuna seed stock back to a "spicy salad mix" I planted a few years ago. The mizuna and the mustard quickly outgrew and overpowered the other greens, which eventually gave up and wilted away. I'm sure there are mixes much better calibrated than the one I tried but, even so, I think it must be near impossible to have every seed germinating at exactly the same moment and growing at exactly the same rate, which is what would have to happen to ensure an overall healthy growth pattern. Tempting as the salad mixes might appear I still prefer to grow two or three different leaf varieties separately and then pick my own mix when harvesting.

Harvesting Greens

A word on harvesting greens: It's important, no, let's make that *essential*, to get the "field heat" out of the greens ASAP! No leaving them out on the deck or kitchen counter for an hour or so, the way I used to do, only to then wonder why the lettuce had turned limp so quickly. I have trained myself, and believe me I don't train easily, to at least submerge greens in icy cold water the very moment they're picked, even if it isn't convenient at that time to thoroughly wash and sort through them. This is a biggie! So fundamentally simple, yet so essential. It's quite interesting to feel how much heat the greens actually release even as they're being submerged and this makes it easier to understand why it's important to cool them off as quickly as possible to ensure the leaves remain crisp.

The effort that goes into growing anything must surely deserve honoring its requirements for harvesting and preparation. Keeping this thought in mind helped me to become less careless, and more diligent, with this process. Generally, I'm not a fan of kitchen gadgets, as they often seem to be more trouble than they're worth. I like to keep things as simple as possible, which is why I mused and pondered on getting a salad spinner for way too long. That's especially true when I think back on all the time I wasted washing and drying greens without one! Now, I think of a salad spinner (see Chapter Eight) as being almost as essential to the home gardener as a trowel. I keep mine in the handiest cupboard and use it pretty much every day throughout the summer and several times a week during the rest of the year.

Thinking Ahead

If washing greens was previously a deterrent to making full use of my salad bed, time was another. Whether I just suck at effective time management or whether, as I suspect, there are just not enough hours in any given day, is debatable; the fact remains that come suppertime, much as I might crave a salad I don't always (almost never do) have the time to stroll out to the garden, sunhat in place, harvest basket in hand, to sniff the roses and gather the fresh greens. Let's not even mention having time enough to wash and prepare them.

Picking enough for several salads when time does allow circumvents this problem. Washed and plate ready, lettuce will keep perfectly well in plastic bags in the fridge and will provide several days' worth of instant salads.

At the very moment I was beginning to write this section on lettuce a friend sent me a picture of greens growing in a rain gutter attached to the side of a building. As we both believe in serendipitous happenstance it was agreed that I should mention this system of growing salad, thereby negating the lack of a garden as an excuse for not growing salad greens. :) I'm not totally sold on the idea of growing greens in rain gutters as I question how often these greens would need watering and fed in such shallow troughs. At least daily would be my guess.

What does appeal to me is the idea of starting seeds, such as peas, indoors, in short lengths of rain gutter, then simply sliding the contents as an oblong plug into a prepared shallow trench outside, once the risk of frost is over and the seeds are well sprouted. I do intend to try this, more out of curiosity than anything else. Stay tuned!

4

Squash & Garlic

No DOUBT IT has become quite apparent by now that I love most vegetables, but even in my crowded arena of favorites, squash tend to roll to the forefront. Not unlike greens, there are many, many varieties to choose from and there are also two main kinds: winter squash and summer squash, which are similar in some ways and in other ways quite different.

SUMMER AND WINTER SQUASH

Similarities

The seeds all look much the same in that they tend to be oval, flattish and on the large size for seeds, usually half to three quarters of an inch (1–2 cm) long. Even as they sprout their first two leaves, winter and summer squash appear to be very similar: sturdy, succulent, and shaped much like the seed they sprouted from. In fact the seed casing is sometimes still attached and keeping the leaves bound together. If, after a couple of days, the leaves haven't been able to cast off this casing it is possible to very gently ease it off and allow the two leaves to separate and open up to adjacent sides.

All squash like soil that is very rich in compost, manure and organics, and they much prefer to be planted in mounds to allow for good drainage. Even though they like lots of moisture they do not like their roots to be waterlogged. They also like the soil to be quite warm and the seeds will refuse to germinate, and might even rot, if the soil is too cold.

Are they starting to sound like they're fussy little critters, more trouble to grow than they're worth? Not so! A couple of buckets of organic nutrients mixed with some soil will create their own mound that just needs to be patted down a bit. The hardest part of growing squash for me is being patient and making sure not to plant before the soil has had chance to warm sufficiently. It is possible to start seeds indoors (or buy transplants) but once squash seeds have germinated outside they grow very quickly and it's been my experience that they catch up and sometimes surpass transplants, which can be very sensitive about being relocated and often go into a "sulk."

Differences

The plants become noticeably different as they begin to grow. Many winter squash form a vine which likes to travel along the ground, sending up stout stalks which are topped with a single large leaf. Winter squash will move through a vegetable plot like an invading army, so it's much better, if possible, to have a dedicated squash patch (that should be rotated each year) or at least to plant them at the perimeter of a bed where the squash vines can travel out into the great beyond, even up trees and onto trellises. Because my soil, after many years of amendments, is now very rich, squash tend to get quite unruly, blocking pathways, etc. I really should nip the ends off all the vines and try to force them to think about producing fruit, but sometimes it's fun to see just how far they will stretch. A mindset not recommended for smaller gardens!

Summer squash on the other hand, while producing similar looking leaves and dominating a fairly large circumference (two to three feet) are not vines, and each leaf bearing stalk can be traced back to the original planting mound. These are large plants and even though, when the tiny seedlings appear it might look like they'll have plenty of room, they probably won't. One of my big mistakes is to allow

SQUASH FLOWERS:

How to Tell Them Apart

It's really not so difficult even though they're both yellow and approximately the same trumpet shape. For starters the female flowers tend to "squat" close to the center or stem of the plant whereas the male flowers stick right up on much longer stems, perhaps to more easily attract the attention of the bees. Female flowers have a small round bump at the base of the flower which, when the flower is fertilized, will swell into a full sized squash, whereas the petals of the male flowers attach directly onto the stem.

overcrowding. It's wasteful and silly but I find it so hard to cull tender young plants that even now I'll let that extra one stay when I really do know better. Two to three plants per mound is almost more than plenty.

Saving Seed

Squash seeds are paradoxically some of the easiest to save, yet also some of the most difficult to regenerate true to type, because different varieties will cross pollinate. Bees love the brilliant yellow, trumpet shaped blossoms of squash plants, and it's fun to watch them crawling in and out, from one flower to another, buzzing ecstatically all the way. If there are different varieties of squash in fairly close proximity their pollens will get mixed because of this frenetic bee activity and will eventually result in a mongrel breed of squash, perfectly edible, but just not what might be expected from the subsequent season's crop. In a large enough garden, where the differing species can be planted far enough apart, this might not happen, but the only way to be truly certain that the seed will remain true to the original plant is to carefully transfer pollen from one flower to another using a small sable brush and then cover the flowers with row cover. I have never done this and probably never will, because it seems too persnickety, but it's the only sure way to ensure that seed will be true to kind.

As if that didn't sound complicated enough, it's also essential to ensure that the flowers chosen for this artificial insemination process are female flowers. Squash plants have both male and female flowers and only the females will bear fruit. The male flowers simply wither and fall off, although I'm told they are quite good harvested, dipped in batter and fried.

Planting Squash

I do hope that wasn't too much information, or that it made squash seem like too much effort, because indeed squash are an especially good choice, especially in a developing garden where the soil throughout is not uniformly perfect. If the mounds they're planted in provide them with enough nutrients, squash will tolerate less than perfect soil around them, just so long as it is well mulched and relatively weed free.

This is actually an effective way to create better soil, when working from sparse beginnings, as the mulch surrounding the squash plants will rot down quite easily. After harvest, the mounds can be levelled onto the mulch and the mixture will gradually become beautifully friable soil. I did this years ago in a couple of places where there was virtually no soil at all, just an overlay of humus on clay, and now these are two of my richest beds. It might sound too good to be true but it happens, mostly because of the dedicated efforts of all the tiny bugs, microbes and nematodes. Much as I love to see the robins return in the spring, I find it much less pleasing to watch them playing tug of war with their breakfast—a big juicy worm. And yes, I have been known to rescue the worm. Sounds silly, I know, but that's how important worms are to the soil.

WINTER SQUASH

Winter squash is particularly satisfying in every way. They're visually very pleasing (I even like to paint pictures of them) and they keep well for several months in a cool, dry place. However, it's best not to store them somewhere they might be forgotten—such as under the bed in the spare room. Not pretty!

Common winter squash are Butternut, Buttercup, Hubbard and Acorn. One of my ultimate comfort foods is curried Butternut soup, but simply quartered, oiled and baked, any winter squash is irresistibly delicious. And the color. Wow! That brilliant orange says it all. Winter squash are a rich source of beta-carotene and omega-3, just what's needed to keep the immune system super strong through the cold and flu season. They're also noted as antioxidants, and as possible aids to regulating blood sugars because of the five B complex vitamins they contain. They have no cholesterol and only deliver around eighty calories per cup. Squash are technically a fruit

because they contain their seed and these seeds, lightly oiled and roasted provide a yummy, healthy, low cal snack. Really! Can't say enough good things about winter squash.

Spaghetti Squash

Another, less usual squash, is the spaghetti squash. Just thinking about them makes me want to have one right now! They're unusual in that, true to their name, the flesh is stringy and once it's baked will fork off the outer skin, appearing to be just like strands of spaghetti. Served with a favorite pasta sauce it tastes amazing, is way more nutritious and has far fewer calories (42 per cup) than typical pasta. I'd still prefer it to regular pasta even it this wasn't so. For some reason I tend to think of them as being more of a summer squash but they are usually referred to as a winter squash and they do grow on a vine.

Pumpkins

Although pumpkins are technically a winter squash, I also tend to think of pumpkins as a sort of bridge between winter and summer squash. Scientifically they are more clearly defined, but in my mind they tend to sit on the fence between summer and winter. They're certainly grossly underestimated and not appreciated half as much as they deserve. I find it quite distressing to see so much waste after Hallowe'en, especially considering how that same nutrition, properly channelled, could be filling hungry bellies and literally saving lives. Much like other squash, they offer a low cal powerhouse of nutrition and yet it's seems to be generally quite acceptable to throw them out ... or throw them at something. I know there might be a limit to how many pies and muffins a family can consume but there are other uses.

Pumpkin pickle for example, was apparently very popular and commonly eaten only a couple of generations ago. It's easy to make, very pleasing to the eye and truly delicious, so it's not hard to understand its erstwhile popularity. It's much more difficult to understand

◄ This spaghetti squash has already crept several feet from its original mound and climbed up into the tomatillo patch.

its fall from grace. My theory, and it's only a theory, is that as the annual frenzy surrounding Hallowe'en increased, so did the sight of discarded pumpkins, carved and left out too long on frosty nights. In turn this proliferated into the notion that pumpkins had only one destiny and that path did not lead to the dinner table. Two caveats here: pumpkins grown specifically for the Hallowe'en market might well have been fed nasty stuff to speed up and increase their growth, and I'm also sure that there are hybrid strains developed specifically for quick growth, rather than taste. Eating or "table" pumpkins are often referred to as "pie pumpkins."

Homegrown is definitely the best way to go and as pumpkins are easy to grow and prolific it's fun to encourage young gardeners to come and tend their own in preparation for the "big day." Scary faces do not need to be carved in, they can be drawn on or applied as felt shapes. There, that's my campaign to save the noble pumpkin from a horrible Hallowe'en fate. Except for one last word: a dollop of mashed pumpkin mixed in with Fido/Fiona's food will eliminate various bowel issues, according to my vet—our dog's vet, I should say. :)

SUMMER SQUASH

Now that I've crossed over my bridge of pumpkins I'm in summer squash space. Not quite that time yet, but it's really nice to close my eyes and anticipate reaching into a jungle of giant leaves, that are allowing just enough sunlight to filter through onto the young, shiny-skinned zucchinis and yellow neck squash waiting to be harvested.

Zucchinis

Summer squash are best harvested young. One of my favorite summer lunches, that takes no more than a couple of minutes to prepare (and let's face it, who wants to spend much time in the kitchen on a wonderfully sunny day?) is a couple of fresh picked "zukes," sliced, seasoned and sautéed with a handful of cherry tomatoes and perhaps topped with a little feta and chopped parsley. These lovely squash are equally delicious eaten raw, chopped in salads that can be either vegetable or fruit based. Fresh young zucchini chopped in a fruit salad resembles pear or apple, especially if the salad has been anointed with some extra juice.

Even though it's best to pick zucchinis sooner rather than later, this is easier said than done as they seem to have an uncanny ability to camouflage themselves among the leaves. Fortunately, larger zucchinis are also yummy and they can be stuffed, baked, fried or shredded into all kinds of muffins and loaves. There's a saying that you should not leave your car unlocked around harvesting time as you're likely to find the backseat loaded up with zucchinis when you return. Yes, it's easy to score a bushel or so of them during peak season because they really are that prolific. So why grow your own? To have that immediate and constant supply of young tender skinned ones. The ones left in cars tend to be the older, thicker-skinned ones.

Other Summer Squash Varieties

I feel I should at least mention yellow neck squash here because they are a common summer squash. I have always found them to be less prolific but then I do tend to concentrate my efforts on the zucchinis, just because they are my favorites. My all-time favorite type of zucchini is called Costata Romanesca and in my estimation it seems to float somewhere between a regular zucchini and a vegetable marrow. Costata Romanesca are always most welcome in my garden, even though they are said not to produce as high a yield as other varieties.

Marrow

Marrow tends to be a catch-all word that can include all summer squash, but in the U.K. it refers more specifically to a larger, more elongated, beige to light green squash. I can still remember my first encounter with one of these strange beasts when I was quite a young child. It was served to me stuffed, with what I don't know, but most probably rice and "mince" (ground beef) and I thought it

Cloves of hard neck garlic break apart around a woody central stem.

was the most amazing thing I'd ever tasted. I don't know whether or not it was a rarity at that time, when menus depended very much on the basic staples such as potatoes . . . and potatoes, but I certainly don't remember ever having another vegetable marrow before the one I grew myself. My memory for once had not played tricks on me and it tasted just as wonderful as I'd remembered from way back when.

GARLIC

Now to spice things up a bit with those tight bound bulbs that have had several claims to fame over the centuries, including the ability to scare away vampires and protect against the Bubonic plague. Garlic! As with most "old wives tales," especially those relating to herbal cures, claims about the curative properties of garlic come from deep-seated wisdom, although the vampire connection has yet to be scientifically substantiated.

Garlic is a powerful antibiotic and immune system booster that is said to improve heart health, reduce the risk of osteoarthritis, help to lower high blood pressure and high cholesterol, and even to combat athlete's foot, all because of its anti-bacterial, anti-fungal properties. The main source of these healing properties is allicin, which is also what gives garlic its distinctive smell. It is only released—well, actually it gets converted from the compound alliin by the enzyme alliinase—when the garlic clove is crushed. This might all sound very complex but it's good to keep in mind. In other words wearing a necklace of whole garlic cloves, as was done in the Middle Ages, will not necessarily provide much protection against the Great Plague, even if it does offer some relief from the fear of vampires, werewolves and other evil spirits. The true healing powers of garlic are only released with the juice.

Growing Garlic

Garlic might seem like an overly ambitious choice for a book that's focussing on garden start-ups and easy grows, especially to anyone who has tried unsuccessfully to produce a respectable garlic harvest. The fact that garlic is not often included in a typical home garden has further added to its aura of mystique. Garlic simply has certain specific requirements, and that does not mean that these requirements are complex or difficult. In fact, contrary to any sly rumors or misconceptions that might be slinking around, garlic is easy to grow, as well as being a healthy and tasty choice. The garlic bulbs are broken up and each individual clove is planted separately, a couple of inches deep and about eight inches apart.

First point simply put, garlic is very slow to grow. Because of this it prefers to be planted in the late fall rather than in early spring. (Some garden centers might well offer garlic bulbs for planting in the spring but they're not really playing fair.)

Harvesting Garlic Scapes

Second point harvesting garlic is actually a two part process. In late July, early August the garlic plant, which up until this point will have looked much like a meagre, flowerless daffodil will produce "scapes." These elegant stems are topped with a delicately pointed seed case which is shaped like a pixie hat. After the scape has reached a height of two to three feet (may be lower with some varieties) the tip, still wearing its cute little pixie hat, will droop and begin to curl, in essence forming a circle about three inches in diameter. Around the time a second coil is forming the scape should be harvested by following the stem down towards its base and cutting it off above the leaves. These scapes are fun to include in flower arrangements but it always seems a shame not to use them all in the kitchen.

How to explain the taste and texture of a garlic scape? Definitely garlicy but milder than the bulbs. They're more substantial than salad onions and perfect for stir-fries and soups, but the bulk of our scapes usually get made into pesto and from there into pastas, sauces and dips. Garlic scapes are really cool and I think I'd love them for their looks alone, even if they didn't taste so good.

SPRING PLANTED GARLIC
Best practice is to always plant garlic in the fall but sometimes life happens and the fall planting of garlic doesn't. If garlic is planted as early as possible in the spring it will still produce a crop. It will mature several weeks later than fall planted garlic and the cloves probably won't be as big, but let's face it, any garlic is better than no garlic, right? Just to be clear, this is not recommended, but it is doable.

▲ This garlic scape harvest is destined to make lots of super tasty pesto.

If the scapes are not harvested the plant will invest all its efforts into producing seed rather than developing bulbs: the scape will uncoil, now standing several feet high, the pixie hat will swell and eventually split open to reveal a sizeable round ball of flowerets, each of which has the potential (in two-three years) to become another garlic bulb. It's worth leaving one scape unharvested just to watch this process and enjoy the attractive flower head that's produced.

Years ago, when I didn't know any better, I planted garlic in the late spring and was very disappointed with what I dug up later that same summer—one small nubby clove as I remember. :(This was enough to make me think of garlic as some exotic that was near impossible to grow around here, when in fact I simply hadn't given it half the time it needed to mature. I don't believe it had even had time to produce scapes and if it had, I certainly didn't harvest them. No wonder there was little to show for my misguided efforts!

Harvesting Garlic

Garlic is actually very easy to grow, it just needs plenty of time. Once the cloves are in the ground—they like rich soil with high organic content—as long as they're well mulched to prevent weeds they can be forgotten about until the scapes form. Several weeks after the scapes have been harvested the bottom two or three leaves of the plant will begin to turn brown and whither, signifying that it's time to dig up the bulbs. Yay! The single clove which was planted will have multiplied into a bundle of at least four or five cloves and perhaps as many as ten or twelve, depending on the variety planted. The bundle of cloves will be perfectly packaged into one garlic bulb. If the papery white skin around the bulb has begun to break open this will be a sign that they should have been harvested slightly earlier. That's okay, they're still good to use but might not keep as long. Bearing in mind that the shelf life of garlic is several months, chances are that any compromised garlic will have been used long before it has a chance to sprout.

Storing Garlic

Once harvested, any excess of dirt can be gently removed from the base of the bulb. The green tops, with bulbs still attached, should be bundled and hung to dry in a cool, dry place. We find the garden shed works well. They must not be forgotten and allowed to freeze as this is heartbreaking—the voice of experience speaking. :(When the tops become husk-like, in a couple of weeks or so, it's safe to assume that the cloves are also well dried and they can be cut off, gently brushed clean (but not washed), then stored in a cool dark place.

▶ Newly harvested hard neck garlic—note the withered lower leaves that indicate it was more than time to harvest.

Braiding is an option for soft necked garlic varieties. If this is the plan, the braiding is done directly after harvesting and before the stems have had a chance to dry out.

There are several varieties of garlic, roughly grouped as hard necked and soft necked. The hard neck variety have woody stems, or necks, running up the center of the bulb and have larger but fewer cloves surrounding the neck. I much prefer this type, even though it's said to have a slightly milder flavor, because it's easier to peel. The soft necked varieties obviously are lacking the woody stem and have more, but smaller, cloves per bulb. These bulbs tend to be more tightly wrapped, are stronger in flavor and store better than hard necked varieties. It's a good idea to plant a few of each variety to determine which is preferred and which is best suited to the local conditions. Also, it's good to remember that garlic is a really good companion plant for most vegetables, as it helps deter blight and acts as a fungicide. However, peas and beans absolutely do not like to be planted near garlic or any members of the allium (onion) family.

5

Beans & Onions

OF THE EASY-TO-GROW plants selected for this book, beans and onions (or to be more precise, legumes and alliums) could be said to represent the easiest and the most difficult to grow. I'm mentioning their more scientific names simply to explain why I'm grouping peas with beans. In the kitchen they might be thought of as two different veggies, yes, but in the garden they're both legumes, members of the same family (*Leguminosae*). Now, if I were to have followed this logic throughout, garlic would be grouped with onions because they're also of the same family, but logic can be over-rated, in my opinion.

Companion Planting

Initially, my choice to have beans and onions sharing a chapter was somewhat arbitrary. However, I came to realize that there is a good reason—these two address the important topic of "companion planting" and the fact that while some plants like to hang out together, others don't. These two don't!

Some symbiotic relationships between plants work perfectly. Squash, corn and beans are probably the most common example of companion planting and have been inter-planted for countless generations as staple foods in Native American farming societies. These "three sisters" form mutual support systems by each satisfying a need of their companions while also fulfilling a need of their own. Corn provides a support for the beans to climb up and the broad squash leaves provide shade for the soil, helping it to remain relatively moist and weed free. This is especially beneficial to the beans, which enrich the soil with nitrogen for the benefit of them all. Corn and squash are native to South and Central America but, interestingly, it is Iroquois legend from around the Great Lakes that tells how these three sisters—corn, beans and squash—came as special gifts from the Great Spirit, and cannot survive without each other. The three sisters are thought of as spiritual beings, and are honored as such with planting ceremonies to ensure an adequate harvest.

Beans and onions represent the antithesis of such a partnership in that they won't thrive in close proximity to each other. Alliums (this family includes chives, garlic and leeks, as well as onions) repel aphids, whitefly and other pests. Most plants enjoy this protection and I tend to plant onions around the perimeter of my garden beds to deter pests from even entering. I just make sure not to plant them near places where I have beans. Beans, on the other hand, seem to be popular neighbors with most plants because they have the ability to enrich the surrounding soil with nitrogen. They're like the kids who go to school with extra treats in their lunch box and are quite prepared to share. Everyone wants to be their friend. Following that analogy, onions would be the big, tough kid who'll protect you from bullies—in this case insect pests—just so long as he's your friend.

Companion planting is a huge topic that can become a bit unwieldly if taken to extremes, but here in a nutshell is the overall rationale: many plants have the ability establish "friendships" or symbiotic relationships while others just don't get along. For example, Alliums (members of the onion family) exude a chemical that inhibits growth in legumes (peas and beans) so naturally legumes don't like being up close and personal with members of the Allium family. A simple fact definitely worth remembering.

That was a bit of a meander down the garden path, so to speak, but it's difficult not to wander off track when there are just so many fascinating and beautiful mysteries constantly at play in the garden. I find it quite magical and it's not difficult to imagine how the English fairy tale, Jack and the Beanstalk, originated from the story telling tradition of the seventeen hundreds.

BEANS

Planting a bean in a paper cup is often the first encounter with this kind of magic, although I doubt that many of those elementary science projects continue on into the lair of giants, once they're taken home. However, beans are the popular choice for such activities because they germinate quickly and, as they're great starters, I'm putting them first in this chapter—ahead of onions, that is.

Pole or Runner Beans

There are two main types of beans. It seems like I've said that already about other veggies, but in this case, with bush beans and pole beans, it's pretty easy to guess the difference, right? Pole beans grow on a vine and need to be supported on some kind of vertical structure which the tendrils of the vines can attach themselves to. Pole beans are especially good when space is limited because they have a small footprint. It's absolutely essential to install the support prior to planting and to ensure that the support is firmly secured. If this support seems like overkill in both size and strength it will probably be just about sufficient when that support is over-burdened with a jungle of luscious beans.

The support can be constructed with culled saplings in the traditional teepee shape (which I really like) or it can be a trellis (definitely not of pressure treated wood) or a cylinder of wire mesh, or a frame or wall with strings, anything in fact for the bean plants to twine around. I stress the need for installation prior to planting because the bean tendrils will grab onto the first thing they touch, whatever that might be, so it's essential that they touch the intended support first. Otherwise, they can end up in an inseparable tangle on

▶ A healthy crop of bush beans waiting to be harvested.

the ground. It's easy to think, *I have a few days before those beans sprout so I'll do that later*, because it's almost a guarantee that "later" should have been "sooner."

Perhaps the most commonly known pole bean is the Scarlet Runner, sometimes planted primarily as an ornamental because of its scarlet blossoms, which humming birds and butterflies just adore. They do also produce an edible bean, but these need to be harvested when they're quite young, before the pod has had a chance to become tough and stringy. The plant is very accommodating and prolific, as well as being visually appealing, so I think it deserves a place in the garden. I make a point of planting some every year even though, from a purely pragmatic viewpoint, another selection might be preferable come harvest time. We also plant Mennonite Purple Stripe, which is an all-purpose (snap, shell, or dry) bean. I have recently discovered that it is listed as being extremely rare by Seeds of Diversity Canada, so seed for this particular bean might not be easy to locate.

Bush Beans

The intended purpose of the beans you plant is of course an important consideration. My main purpose for beans is to use them fresh as "snap" beans, so-called because a truly fresh bean pod should be crisp enough to snap. However, food security is also a consideration, and therefore beans that dry well are also important to me. Most beans are not equally good at being all things to all people, but there are several multi-purpose strains available. And as if it wasn't enough to have to decide on their main purpose, there's also the decision of which color to plant: yellow, green or purple. Decisions! Decisions!

It really is best, at least when starting off, to decide on not more than two varieties. I would suggest that one of these be a bush bean variety, if only because they tend to mature a couple of weeks earlier than pole beans. Also, I find them to be crisper (they really do snap rather than bend) and more tender. They are certainly delicious, but generally the harvest is not as on-going as with pole beans. I estimate two generous gatherings from each bush bean plant before the supply diminishes. This can be somewhat offset by staggered planting—planting a limited number of seeds over several consecutive weeks rather than planting the whole crop at the same time, but as our Nova Scotia growing season is short I haven't found this to work so well for me.

Inoculant

When it comes to planting beans, the word "inoculant" will no doubt come up sooner or later. An inoculant contains bacteria that create nitrogen fixing nodules on the roots of legumes. Time was when I didn't bother using an inoculant, considering it to be an unnecessary, time-consuming frill. This was really foolish of me. Inoculating legumes fits effortlessly into the process of planting because the seed will already be damp after a day's soak in water. Yes, it's best to soak seeds but equally important to ensure that planting will happen within a couple of days. Left too long soaking, the seeds will rot. This I know for certain. :(

The inoculant, which has the appearance of finely powdered charcoal, has a limited shelf life and is only viable for one season so there's no point in skimping with the intent of saving some for the next year, especially as soil can't be over-seeded with inoculant. It can be simply sprinkled in the trench where the peas or beans are to be planted or each seed can be coated separately, which is much easier than it sounds. The inoculant is put in a lidded jar and the damp seed is rolled around in the jar until coated, which takes only a second or two. I take the jar outside and plant the coated seed directly from it. Inoculant is one hundred per cent natural in that it comes from dried peat containing cultures of beneficial bacteria. The packets will seem to contain minimal amounts but $5.00 will coat around eight pounds of seed. It's best to avoid over-buying because of its limited shelf life.

▲ Pea vines may look delicate, but once their tendrils connect with something they hold on tight.

Who knew there was so much to say about growing beans ... and I'm just scratching the surface here, hoping to give enough information to ensure that growing legumes will be a truly satisfying experience. Those little kids carrying their single bean sprout home usually appear to be so proud and excited about what they've grown and I think all gardeners should be able to keep that feeling alive within themselves, no matter how experienced they become.

To rewind, I guess I could just have said, *A bean is a bean, is a bean and if the soil is warm and moist enough it will grow and quite probably produce more beans*, but what fun would that have been? And I wouldn't have the opportunity of bragging up the nutritional importance of dried beans. The American Diabetes and the American Heart Associations both flag dried beans as a key food group for preventing disease and promoting good health. At only one hundred and fifteen calories per half cup, beans deliver eight grams of protein, lots of complex carbohydrates, almost no fat and lots of vitamin B along with various important minerals.

Peas

Peas are similar to beans in their nutritional content but, unlike beans that prefer (actually insist upon) warm soil, peas want their soil to be much cooler, which is why they need to be planted much earlier than beans. Peas also come in various types but most of them require support to climb up. Edible pod peas such as snow and snap peas are my favorites but here's the rub, split pea soup is a family favorite so I need to plant two kinds of peas if I also want to grow some sizeable pods, packed with peas that will dry and store well.

Planting Peas

The best way to plant peas is in a shallow trench of rich, friable soil. As the first green shoots emerge the trench can be gradually filled by simply encouraging the sides of the trench to cave in towards the center. This way the roots of the peas will eventually be covered with three to four inches of soil, without the delicate first shoots having to try and force their way up through that same weight of soil, which they might not be able to do. The deeper roots will be better able to keep cool during the heat of summer.

Harvesting

It's important to avoid touching the leaves of peas, and especially of beans, when they're wet, as this tends to spread fungal diseases. Directly after rain or early in the morning before the sun has had time to dry off the dew (and, in my location, the sea mist) are not good times to harvest or cultivate. Fungal diseases are also spread by the wind so they are quite likely to happen sooner or later, and diseased plants should be removed immediately. Any seed saved from infected plants is perfectly edible but should not be saved for replanting.

ONIONS

It's interesting that I left onions until the last. I wonder if I have been subconsciously avoiding them because they are probably the staple crop I have had the most varied success with. I even considered leaving them out altogether but it didn't seem fair to steer anyone away from the delightful convenience of a constant supply of fresh green onions (sometimes referred to as scallions). During their initial growth stage small onion bulbs sprout green shoots which can be pulled and eaten, no problem. It's growing these same onions through to maturity which is more challenging, but more on this topic below.

What is the difference between scallions and green onions, anyway? It's so negligible that I think of them as being interchangeable and for the purposes of this chapter they certainly can be, but for the record: scallions are usually offered for sale in the grocery stores as "green onions" whereas properly speaking green or spring onions actually have a small, round onion already forming at their base,

▲ Onions, young or mature, red, white or green, all will add a little extra pizzazz to most savory dishes.

and have a slightly stronger flavor than scallions. "Real" scallions are another variety. They are straight sided and show no intention of swelling to form a round onion shape, big or small.

Planting Onions

Onions can be started from seed but this is a lengthy procedure and it's far easier to start onions from "sets," which are small bulbs, usually sold in net bags of a hundred. They can go in the ground really early and if planted every two weeks throughout the spring, they'll provide an on-going harvest. A hundred might seem like a lot but this is one instance where more might indeed be better, and two hundred is likely a more reasonable amount. They're so useful that a typical household could easily use that many, especially when they're on the doorstep and ready for pulling. And that's not even considering having a supply of winter onions. These are the critters that give me trouble. Instead of forming a nice round bulb at the base, the tops often refuse to die off but choose instead to grow into giant green onions with a not-so-secret plan to flower and produce seed.

Growing Mature Onions

For a nice round onion to form, the green top needs to wither and die off, draining its substance into the bulb and leaving enough time for the bulb to mature and develop a tough outer skin. This process is related to the number of daylight hours available to the plant and there are long, medium and short day varieties of onion strains. In most of North America, the long-day strains, such as Walla Walla are what needs to be planted. (There are other long-day strains but I just think that name is so cool, I had to choose it!) As they mature the bulbs will push up out of the ground and any mulch that surrounds them should be moved back to leave the tops of the onions clear. Onions should never be mounded over with soil, although they are sometimes planted in mounds to ensure good drainage. This might give the impression that they like to be covered with soil when in fact the opposite is the case.

Harvesting Onions

It's essential to "cure" onions before storing as this will toughen up the outer skin. First spread them out in the sun for a couple of days to thoroughly dry them off so any dirt can be brushed away, then leave them in a well ventilated, cool place for a further couple of weeks before storing in mesh bags or hampers.

Ulysses S. Grant was said to have declared, "I will not move my army without onions!" He obviously knew that onions serve as a good disease preventative, as well as an aid to maintaining good health.

6

Tomatoes & Cucumbers

THE FACT THAT I haven't yet mentioned tomatoes and cucumbers is doubtless starting to seem like a massive omission because, surely, aren't they what everyone wants to grow in their garden? Well yes, they are probably two of the most popular picks for the home gardener and, I suspect, two of the more common sources of disappointment. And one thing I don't want to do, ever, is to discourage anyone from growing their own food.

Sure, once we've enjoyed a couple of fabulous harvests, a crop failure or two isn't as hard to take, but if you've never grown anything before, a single "no show" or "wimp out" can easily fertilize an attack of Black Thumb syndrome. Truth is, Black Thumb, much like Writer's Block, doesn't really exist. It's merely a figment conjured up by that critical adult voice that's always trying to deep-six our brightest dreams. It makes me want to cry when I hear people convincing themselves that they have not a green but a black thumb. There is no such thing!

Plants inherently want to grow. This is an indisputable rule of nature. It just happens that if they don't get exactly what they want or need, whether in terms of water, light or food, then they will sulk. It's a human trait that somehow got passed on to plants. (Just joking.) Becoming a competent gardener, or even a good one, is simply about acquiring the knowledge required to cater to each plant's particular needs. It's all quite straightforward and nothing to do with the color of one's thumb.

Initially, I didn't want to include tomatoes or cucumbers in my main picks because this book focuses on fail-safes, plants that are not high maintenance and that, from my experience, have a fairly high tolerance for human error and will grow just about anywhere. While being relatively easy, tomatoes and cucumbers are not totally fail-safe in these parts.

TOMATOES

Tomatoes need time, not only to form fruit, but also to ripen up. Some years I've had magnificent success planting outside but in a short, lackluster summer, such as we often experience, I've simply ended up with bushels of green tomatoes, only some of which will agree to ripen indoors, shedding much of their flavor along the way. Fortunately we have a greenhouse which enables us to produce a fair crop of tomatoes "under glass" but I'm working on the assumption that most readers aren't so lucky, so I'm just not going there. They also need staking, and certainly around here they definitely need to be started early.

We like to save seed and generate our own plants, which is relatively easy with tomatoes, but once again, that is not a topic for this book. I will however touch on the basics of growing tomatoes for all those lucky enough to have a warm, sheltered spot and the guarantee of a relatively long and sunny summer. So here goes:

Choosing Varieties

Tomato plants are vine-like, either determinate or indeterminate. In theory, an indeterminate tomato will keep on growing and growing and producing fruit here and there along the way, until something kills it off—most likely a drop in temperature or a fungal disease. Tomatoes are not at all frost tolerant, which makes sense considering that they originated in Central America. (They are actually in the nightshade family, which includes peppers and potatoes.) It's best to

nip off all but four or five of the side shoots (called trusses) but not the central (terminal) stem of an indeterminate plant, once it reaches a certain size, in order to encourage it to set better fruit. Otherwise, it might just put all its energy into travelling the world, with the attitude that it's going to live forever, so what need is there to produce fruit, i.e. seed?

Determinate plants will grow to a certain height, two or three feet, and then concentrate on producing fruit. This means that the crop tends to ripen all at once. This is great if the plan is to can spaghetti sauce but not so good for occasional eating spread throughout the season. The perfect solution is to have a couple (or more) of each type to ensure an ongoing supply as well as a sizeable harvest for processing.

Cherry tomatoes tend to fill both of these requirements in the sense that they produce a dozen or more small tomatoes on a single stem. The plants also tend to be slightly more compact and less unwieldy, depending on variety. I particularly like cherry tomatoes because I find them to be sweeter, and I seem to have better success with them.

"Patio" tomatoes are yet another variety of tomato plant, created specifically to be grown in a container in a relatively small space. If we were comparing dogs to tomato plants I would say the patio tomato is akin to a small lap dog, whereas the determinate plant is more like a well behaved Labrador and the indeterminate plants are high energy, irrepressible sheep herders that run around all over the place.

Actually, the very first step in growing tomatoes is to decide what varieties to plant. And this step might indeed be the most difficult as they all have slightly different claims to fame. Reading this section in a seed catalog can be particularly dangerous! We tend to pick heritage and open pollinated varieties but once in a while we try a completely different variety, just because we might be missing something outstanding that is begging to become our next, best favorite. I don't like to recommend specific varieties because what works

◀ This cherry tomato plant was more than happy to hang out all summer on a south facing deck, supplying tasty treats to anyone who happened by.

brilliantly on our little island might not do half so well elsewhere. What works best, I think, is to buy from a local source, whether for plants or seeds, and most definitely from a small, family run greenhouse rather than a grocery store garden center.

Tending Tomatoes

Tomato plants need staking. It's been my experience that the typical wire "tomato cages" are never quite sturdy enough to support a healthy tomato plant and one wooden stake is not enough either, and no, I'm not talking about vampires. Those tender little transplants with three or four leaves will quite rapidly transform into a sprawling, heavy-limbed mass of exuberant growth that is likely to outpace its own strength. It's very discouraging to have a branch that is so loaded down with fruit that it cracks off and withers before the fruit has had chance to ripen.

My main concern in encouraging anyone to grow tomatoes is the susceptibility of these plants to various fungal diseases. I wondered if I was being a bit paranoid here. Was it simply that I live in an area where the sea mist can roll in on the sunniest of days, with little or no warning, which doesn't help at all in the battle to keep various diseases at bay? But no, I went to the Cornell University site (vegetablemdonline.ppath.cornell.edu—which is wonderful by the way) and discovered that there are actually way more threats to tomatoes than I could even have imagined. I'm surprised that we manage to grow any at all!

Planting Tomatoes

This next bit you'll just have to trust me on, even though it might seem counterintuitive. When transplants are being transferred to their permanent summer home in the garden, or in a spacious planter, it's really beneficial to have as much of the stem as possible covered with soil, especially if the transplants have grown somewhat "leggy" in their previous environment. The best way to do this is to lay the plant on its side and bury the stem, leaving only the leaves

▲ Just a very small sampling of the many, many tomato varieties available.

exposed. The buried stem will sprout roots and of course a stronger, more extensive root system will result in a much healthier plant.

Watering

Tomatoes like to be watered deeply, that is, at their roots rather than on their leaves. So once a week, give them a really good soaking around the base, unless of course the weather has been extremely hot and dry, in which case a midweek watering might be needed, especially if the plants look at all droopy. Any excess of water after a dry spell will cause the fruit to split open, which invariably leads to wasted fruit. It's as if the skin can't expand rapidly enough to accommodate the bloated flesh so it splits open. I think it's akin to that post festive feast syndrome that humans sometimes feel like they're experiencing. :) Uneven watering can also lead to blossom end rot.

Pruning

Tomato plants also need pruning on an ongoing basis. As the plant matures suckers start to grow at the crotch of the main branches (trusses). These suckers will yes, suck a lot of energy from the plant, the result being less and smaller fruit. It's much easier to identify and remove these suckers when they are just starting to grow. Once they've formed into a healthy looking branch it's a little scary and I always find myself wondering if I'm snipping off the wrong branch.

Soil Requirements

I realize I've sort of worked backwards on this one, dealing with the mature plant and all its idiosyncrasies first and now ending up with best practice planting. Who knows, perhaps I was subconsciously trying to steer people away from growing tomatoes and kudos for everyone who is refusing to be deterred! So to my final point, which is, in fact, the primary step. (That's weird!) Soil requirements: much like most veggies tomatoes like well-drained soil with lots of organic content that is friable (crumbly) and not too acidic (5.8 – 7.0 pH is best). However, soil too rich in nitrogen will result in massive overgrowth of foliage and not so much fruit. It is possible to draw excess nitrogen from the soil with the addition of wood chips but this can be tricky and not necessarily recommended for anything but extreme conditions. Mulching with red or black plastic works well with tomatoes. It helps warm the soil and also helps impede the spread of some of the soil borne pathogens which spread several diseases.

CUCUMBERS

So, why don't cucumbers grow well for me? Well, for one thing, I think they know that I'm not crazy about them and that I personally much prefer zucchinis. Of course I suppose it might also be that because of the above I don't take as much care of them as I should. Hmmm?

FEEDING TOMATOES

Tomato plants are heavy feeders and remind me of teenagers going through a typical growth spurt. Not only are they voracious, they also have rather defined tastes which tend to revolve primarily around these elements:

Nitrogen a goodly portion is needed to promote healthy growth but too much can causes the plant to produce luxurious leaf but not much fruit.

Phosphorus bone meal is an effective way to introduce phosphorus. A deficiency will manifest in stunted growth and faded color on the lower leaves.

Potassium kelp meal and wood ash are both good ways to add this as tomatoes do have a relatively high requirement.

Calcium crushed egg shells and bone meal are both good sources for this. A calcium deficiency results in blossom end rot, which is a blackening of the base of the tomato.

Magnesium can be added with a pinch of Epsom salts. It plays an essential role in photosynthesis and also in the plants ability to absorb calcium. A lack of magnesium results in a sickly looking plant with yellow leaves. Too much binds up calcium so the plant can't access it.

Unfortunately, I have probably just given enough information to cause a lot of trouble. It is not a good idea to be sprinkling a bit of this and a bit of that, and perhaps a bit more for good measure, the

way I used to do. In fact that is the worst approach because adding one element might well disrupt the balance of another, equally important element in the soil, which would be highly detrimental. Just as an example, potassium needs to be kept balanced with calcium and magnesium or else! It's by far safer to feed the plants often and just lightly with a weak compost tea and perhaps a sprinkle of bone and blood meal around the base once or twice during the growing season. Only when the plants are looking decidedly unhealthy should more radical steps be taken.

▲ Pickling (center), English (right) and "slicing" (left)—all cucumbers, but with distinct differences.

When I was a kid, growing up in a North of England mill town, cucumber was sold by the inch. Seriously! I can remember watching one of the neighborhood housewives trying to decide whether she wanted two, two and a half or three inches of cuke while the patient (but growing less so by the moment) green grocer kept sliding the knife fractionally back and forth, trying to locate the sweet spot. The quintessentially British cucumber sandwiches (with the crusts removed of course) truly were considered to be quite a delicacy. And why so?

Partly I'm sure because cucumbers need sun and warmth, both of which were often in short supply where I grew up, so they were typically grown in a greenhouse. They still like sun and warmth but I suspect that some of the newer strains are slightly less demanding than the pampered English cucumbers of my past.

Choosing Varieties

Not unlike tomatoes, the range of choices available these days can be daunting, but they basically fall into two categories: slicing or pickling . . . or, field or hot-house, depending on how you want to slice them. :) Cucumbers can grow from four to fourteen inches long but a strain that has been programmed to stay small (pickling cukes) will not grow a whole lot larger, no matter how long it's left on the vine. It will simply turn yellow and soft.

Why so many choices? Perhaps the easiest way to answer this is to read some of the descriptions from a popular seed catalog: *long-time standard, extra early and extra heavy yield, vigorous, compact space saver, spineless and burpless, very long and thin skinned, sweet and crisp*—the list goes on and on. There's even a strain that's actually meant to be white and another that's meant to grow round and yellow. I think I already mentioned my aversion to veggies that have been drained of their natural color, so it's a given that any bloated misshapen cukes in *my* garden simply means they got tired of waiting to be harvested and decided to move on to the final stage of their life cycle. Cucumbers need to be harvested very regularly, every other day at their peak, as they mature very quickly and can double in size almost overnight.

Needless to say neither the white nor the yellow strains of cucumber would be my pick but I'm sorely tempted by a variety called "Socrates." I just don't think I can resist, with a name like that, and I'm already imagining myself in the greenhouse, perhaps with the gentle patter of a shower to provide the background music, as this venerable vine and I discourse on the meaning of life.

Still in the seed catalogs, it's interesting to note that degrees of disease resistance are listed in every glowing description, which tends to support my experience, which is that cucumbers are more than a tad vulnerable to various fungal conditions. The list is long!

Now I need to come up with some glowingly enthusiastic words on growing cucumbers for everyone who loves cucumbers and are determined to grow their own, and doubtless will with huge success!

Growing Vertically

I'm really finding this hard! Well, they're very amenable to growing vertically, which is great because this means they have a very small footprint and therefore take up very little space. I've also seen it suggested that when growing vertically they are less prone to disease as the air circulation is far better than around plants sprawled on ground, and certainly they don't tend to yellow on the bottom side when not lying on the ground.

We have had the most success growing them up a trellis, as long as they're well secured. And yes, it is nice to be able to add one to a salad once in a while, or slice up a dish with some wine vinegar and fresh herbs. Of course if you like Raita, whether the traditional Indian version which has a heavy emphasis on cilantro or the minty version—reminding me of another almost too easy to grow herb that I almost neglected to mention—growing cucumbers is a must.

So yes, absolutely, if you like cucumbers, grow them, no matter how new you are to growing your own food. A couple of things to keep in mind: cucumbers require a lot of water to grow well but moisture on their leaves tends to encourage mold and fungus issues, so it is definitely best to water at the base, and in the morning so that the ground has a chance to dry out before nightfall. Two further considerations: it is thought that spraying the leaves with compost tea will help inhibit the spread of diseases typical to cucumbers and, finally, it's very important not to work around the plants when the leaves are damp, as this definitely increases their susceptibility.

COMPOST TEA

Most plants like to have a good cuppa' once in a while, just like we do, but their taste requirements differ considerably from ours! First off, I need to stress that I'm using the term "tea" very loosely here— some would argue that to make true compost tea requires special equipment, in the form of a bubbler or aerator. In my book, steeping any combination of compost, manure, green waste or straw, in water for a few days will make a potent brew that plants will love. I have some mighty dynamic accumulators growing in my garden (plants with powerful tap roots that reach deep into the soil to bring up micro nutrients) and the top growth from these plants, coarsely chopped and steeped, is one of the best ways to access these nutrients. It's important to remember that compost tea is very potent and needs to be diluted, at least six to one but, playing safe, ten to one.

7

Herbs

HERBS COULD VERY easily become an obsession—they are so numerous and diverse; plus, much of the folkloric wisdom that enfolds them can now be scientifically supported. The use of herbs dates back beyond Biblical times and their aromatic and curative properties have been widely utilized for generations. Some of the old herbals lay some pretty heavy responsibilities on these tender little plants, attributing them with the power to heal most common ailments, as well as offer protection from all manner of evils and ensure a happy and productive love life.

Quaint as some folk wisdom might seem it's important to remember that many modern medicines are based upon the chemical compounds found in herbs. For instance, Valerian is the forerunner of Valium. One of the neighborhood cats was well aware of its calming effects and I'd often see him in my garden, blissfully gnawing away on the exposed root of a Valerian plant. When I'd go to shoo him off he'd saunter (sometimes even stagger) away, totally zonked, mewing his feline version of *Peace, Baby, Peace.*

Herbs have such a wide and fascinating range of attributes that entire gardens, not to mention voluminous books, are dedicated entirely to herbs. However, for the purposes of this book, I'm going to restrict myself to only three, or four and maybe just a couple more,

▲ Cooking with fresh herbs is super easy with this three tier planter and several herb pots right by the kitchen door.

which might seem unfair (verging on immoral even), especially after such a buildup!

PARSLEY

Time was, not so long ago, when parsley was never taken seriously. It tended to be thought of as a frill, a little sprig of garnish that more often than not got left on the side of the plate. Crazy! Especially considering that 3.5 oz. (100g) of parsley is a rich source of vitamins C and A (twice the recommended daily intake) along with other vitamins, as well as being high in iron and other minerals. It contains a remarkable amount of vitamin K, which promotes healthy bones, and it also works as a powerful diuretic, so is really useful in treating fluid retention and urinary tract infections.

The intense green color of parsley reflects its high content of chlorophyll, which is an antiseptic that helps ward off bad breath and other odors. It's interesting to note that parsley, originally native to the Mediterranean regions, is often paired with garlic. Gremolata, a popular Italian garnish, consists of nothing but garlic and parsley minced together, with just a little zest of lemon. Serving it raw or added right at the end of any cooking process, ensures that the vitamin content of parsley is not much diminished.

Parsley tastes really good and leaves the palate feeling clean and refreshed. I like to have a couple of big planters full of parsley right outside the kitchen door, so I can reach out and grab a bunch whenever I need some. I also grow several plants throughout the garden beds for when I'm preparing dishes that require an extra-large amount. There are two main varieties—curly and broad leafed (also called Italian parsley). I prefer the curly variety as it always seems to be crisper, brighter in color and more robust. Technically parsley is a biennial but I've found it rarely survives the harsh winters around here and that it's best to re-seed every year. Parsley is very slow to germinate and needs to be started indoors, early in the season.

SUMMER SAVORY

Another popular herb (traditional to Maritime Canada, as I'm told) is Savory, also known as Summer Savory. And yes, there is a Winter Savory which apparently has a stronger flavor and is a semi-hardy perennial (but not hardy enough for my neck of the woods—zone 6A). Summer savory is an annual that can be seeded directly outside or started inside in seed trays.

Its flavor is more pungent than parsley and I like it best in chowders and stews, although it's also popular in vegetable dishes and especially with beans, as it's said to alleviate flatulence. Savory has antiseptic, antibacterial, antifungal, and antioxidant properties and is also crazy high in iron, calcium and manganese, as well as A, B-6 and C vitamins. Obviously it's not just the taste that makes this herb a good choice.

The plant grows like a little bush, usually about twelve to sixteen inches high, with small, spikey leaves and tiny lavender colored flowers. It dries well, keeping most of its flavor, which is a definite plus as many herbs lose a lot of their taste during the drying process. The leaves, once dry, strip off the branches quite easily and the woody stems have a pleasing aroma. One year I had a lot of woody stems left after I'd stripped the leaves off them and was able to shape them into circles which I decorated with little packages of other herbs I'd grown and dried. These "herb wreathes" made sweet little gifts at Christmas time.

DILL

Dill has a long and colorful history. It's mentioned in the Book of Matthew as a means of paying tithe, and in the Middle Ages it was thought to protect against witchcraft. Also, when infused in wine, it was said to enhance "passion," although I can't help wondering if that was not just an effect of the wine! The leaves, flowers and seeds are all used to flavor a host of dishes; its uses go way beyond pickles.

Years ago I promised to take something a little sumptuous to a brunch that a friend of mine was hosting for a rather uppity relative. Unfortunately, I forgot about the brunch until an hour or so prior to the event. This happened right around the time I had just met my dear husband Calum and I think we must have been living purely on love because the cupboards were totally devoid of brunch makings, sumptuous or otherwise, and the only thing in the freezer was an ancient, ice-encrusted salmon that I'd intended to feed to the cats. Amazingly, it made a big splash at the brunch, floating in a white sauce, heavily flavored with fresh dill and decorated with dill flowers and nasturtiums. The dish looked and smelt so majestic that I

think I could have replaced the salmon with an old sock and no one would have noticed. (I doubt the taste would have been much altered either.) It's amazing what the power of suggestion and the liberal use of fresh herbs can do! :)

It's just as lovely to have fresh dill available for less extreme circumstances. I like the delicate, feathery leaves chopped into salads, dressings and sauces, and especially on new potatoes with butter. Yum! A couple of years ago we discovered a variety called "Bouquet" that concentrates on producing lots of leaf as opposed to shooting up giant flower heads and not supplying much leaf at all. I like to plant both varieties because, much as I like to have a substantial supply of the leaves, I'm also quite fond of the look of dill flowers, both outside in the garden and inside, in a vase. I enjoy wafting my hand through them as I pass by, just to enjoy the fresh dilly smell.

While it's perhaps not quite such a nutritional powerhouse as the previously mentioned herbs, 3.5 oz. of dill supplies two and a half times the daily requirement of vitamin A and one hundred and forty percent of vitamin C, along with lots of iron and manganese. And as if looks and nutrition weren't good enough reasons for planting dill, it's also a useful companion plant, in that its showy flower heads attract beneficial insects.

NB carrots and tomatoes, or any of the other member of the nightshade family (peppers, potatoes and eggplant) do not like to be planted near dill.

CILANTRO/CORIANDER

I have a strange love/hate relationship with cilantro. Sometimes I find myself thinking, *Wow! That tastes so good.* And then at other times I'm not even sure if I like the taste at all, which is part of the reason why I couldn't decide whether to include it or not. The *when I like it, I like it a lot* part of me won through and I'm glad because cilantro really is a neat little plant, almost like two plants in one actually, because the seed of cilantro is coriander. This can be a little

◀ Dill flowers are beautiful in the garden and very useful in the kitchen.

confusing because in herbals the plant is called coriander, whereas in seed catalogs and in the grocery stores it's generally referred to as cilantro. Both names designate the same plant, which has pungent leaves that look a lot like Italian parsley but with much finer teeth on the edge of the leaf. The coriander seed is perfectly round and about the size of a small lentil. It is commonly seen in pickling spices, and is popular in East Indian cuisine.

This "split-personality" herb can prove frustrating when it's planted for its leaves because it often insists on bolting, intent on producing coriander seeds. Cilantro really objects to warm summer weather, which is why it opts to transform itself, produce seed and be done. So, for a plentiful supply of cilantro leaves, seeding needs to take place in late summer so the cilantro leaves will be able to enjoy the cooler fall days.

Cilantro is commonly used in Thai and Moroccan food and often paired with lime, whereas coriander is more synonymous with East Indian food. Coriander is mentioned in early Sanskrit and Egyptian writings, and in the Middle Ages was thought of as an aphrodisiac and included in love potions. Given the amount of times love potions are mentioned in the old herbals it's hard to know whether our forefathers were particularly lustful or just very unappealing and in need of all the help they could get!

The nutritional and curative properties of cilantro/coriander are quite amazing and include treatments for skin and stomach disorders, high blood pressure, high blood sugar, anemia and eye infections. It also delivers healthy amounts of vitamins and minerals.

For a while the curative properties attributed to herbs seemed so broad and varied that it made me skeptical, until I learned how healing aids are classified in Chinese medicine: as inferior, middle and superior. The inferior class align most closely with Western medicine in that they deal solely with one symptom. Those in the middle range strengthen a broad range of systems within the body and the superior ones work to keep the whole body in optimum health. Of course, this method of classification raises the obvious question: why would I want to go with a middle or inferior grade treatment when I can choose the complete or superior healing system? Believing as I do that everything in this amazing universe is intricately designed to maintain a perfect balance, this subtle shift to seeing herbs through the lens of Chinese medicine makes it much easier for me to believe that one little plant can help keep my blood and bones, as well as my eyes and digestive system, healthy. I have learned to value my herbs for much more than just their taste and even though I might not understand exactly how they work, I've come to think of them as an extra blessing on the meal.

CHIVES

Shame on me! How could I have neglected to mention chives? These beautiful little plants certainly deserve better. They have so many pluses and I can't think of a single negative thing to say about them. They are virtually self-tending and very loyal in that they tend to poke their way up every spring, no matter how much they've been neglected. I have several clumps that re-seeded themselves on a pebble pathway years ago and seem to be blissfully unaware that they are growing in a most inhospitable place.

Chives could be treasured simply for the wonderful display of bright purple pompoms they produce when they flower (usually late May early June), but actually their main claim to fame should be that they are super useful in the kitchen because of their delicate onion flavor. They will complement just about any food, and their bright green color stays even after cooking. I especially like to include them with potatoes (hashed, mashed, baked or re-fried), eggs (omelets, frittatas or simply scrambled), dressings, dips, salads and the list could go on: butter, pastas, garlic bread... but I'm pretty certain I've made my point. Chives rule!

What makes them extra cool is that in addition to the multi-functionality of their green spikey "leaves" the flowers themselves

▲ Year after year, with little to no attention, this clump of chives pops up to delight in a quiet corner of the garden.

are also edible and make a lovely garnish, not to mention a unique gourmet vinegar. And, the more they're cut the more they grow. It is in fact better to keep cutting the flowers and greens through the season, so that they don't fulfill their cycle and die off early.

In the garden they work well as companion plants by deterring bugs, helping to keep them away from other plants, and because chives are fairly tough and vigorous they don't mind being dug up and split into two or more clumps. Because of this, it's easy enough to generate a protective barrier around the veggie plot.

Folkloric wisdom dictates that a few clumps of chives planted by the door will deter evil spirits and help keep the inhabitants healthy.

I'm not sure about that, but I do know that having a couple of clumps growing close to the kitchen door, either in pots or directly in the ground, is very convenient.

Chives contain a significant amount of vitamins A and C, and are noted as having diuretic qualities. They're up and ready for harvesting when not very much else is and they're perennials. Surely chives deserve a place in every garden. If there's no garden they can be potted up on the deck, and if there's no deck or doorstep, even on a sunny window ledge close by.

MINT

Mint is perhaps the easiest thing of all to grow. So much so, in fact, that rather than tending it, I seem to spend more time ripping it out, which must sound like a strange approach for someone who professes to love the taste of mint. Mint, much like a bossily aggressive goat, needs to be put in its place every so often, otherwise it will totally commandeer any space that is relatively rich and moist. I once met someone who claimed she had managed to kill off all her mint and who was delighted to be given as many plants as I was equally delighted to offload. (I did warn her!)

There are so many varieties of mint, and maybe some of the designer strains are less determined, but I grow three basics that all have roots that resemble the innards of a high voltage switch box. Fortunately, most of my mint is thriving in places where nothing else is hoping to, but every so often even those patches need to be severely culled so they don't start choking each other out and deciding to migrate.

I have chocolate mint, spearmint and regular old traditional mint, the kind that was grown mainly for mint sauce and mint jelly when I was growing up: condiments I believed simply had to accompany roast lamb. Mint is really easy to dry and makes a lovely tea, which is mostly what I use it for, and it's actually quite high in vitamins, especially C, and certain minerals, as well as being a digestive aid. I love

▲ Mint gone wild!

the smell of mint in the garden and in bouquets. During my rounds in the garden I usually pick a leaf or two to chew on. It's actually one of my standard delights of an early summer morning, and certainly a garden would seem bereft without the scent of mint.

The important thing is, and this deserves special billing, be sure to plant mint in a restrictive area; absolutely, definitely not as part of a veggie plot; and perhaps best in a large (escape-proof) planter. The word here is, yes, definitely grow mint but treat it like a rather dangerous prisoner who just happens to have a very likeable personality.

In the Kitchen

8

Gifts & Gizmos

getting started in the kitchen

I **FEEL QUITE WELL** equipped to write this chapter, not because I have any pretensions about being a super-chef (or even a fair-to-middlin' cook) but for exactly the opposite reasons. I never was much good at cooking and what's more, this fact did not bother me one bit. I found kitchen work to be boring and totally uncreative—*a chore*, when I was being polite, and *a complete waste of time*, when I was being honest.

So what changed? How did my relationship with food preparation get flipped upside down? Well, for one thing, growing your own food pretty much ensures a lifetime membership in the slow food movement. I'd always been interested in healthy eating and this interest expanded as a natural extension of my veggie plots. Food preparation just became so much more interesting, especially as everything homegrown comes to take on a special significance, along with its superlative flavors.

I've always enjoyed exquisitely prepared food but had relegated it to pricey restaurants and the tables of friends who had nothing better to do than spend hours in the kitchen. Such was my dilemma: wanting to enjoy beautiful meals and producing the ingredients for such meals, but not having the expertise or inclination to prepare them.

Once again Necessity, that wonderful mother, who so often gives me that extra shove in the right direction, can take some of the credit for my epiphany and the rest goes to my wonderful husband, who's still a much better cook than I am, even though I'm catching up fast. Me! Writing on efficiency in the kitchen will seem like a strange concept, especially to anyone who knew me way back when, who might now be thinking that pigs are quite likely to be flying soon!

To my on-going amazement, kitchen stuff is not difficult, doesn't have to be tediously time-consuming and can, in fact, become quite interesting. Hard to believe, but this was a huge learning curve for me. My dislike of food preparation, I now realize, was in part due to a lack of suitable tools. Anyone who has tried to cut up vegetables with a dull knife will know how frustrating that is. Unfortunately, the price of a really good kitchen knife can be equally distressing. But a good knife (preferably three) is totally essential and the truth is it's better to have one good knife, rather than a fancy looking block sprouting a whole collection of mediocre knives. A good knife is one that stays sharp for more than just a couple of cuts—but then, even the best of knives requires sharpening once in a while so it's a really good idea to have some form of knife sharpener on hand. I'm sure everyone has seen images of some famous chef or other dragging his knife back and forth along a "wand" of coarsely ridged steel. It takes a while to perfect that kind of professional flourish. Using a ceramic disc knife sharpener, while perhaps less impressive, might be a better option. Obviously, a poorer quality knife will require sharpening more frequently.

NECESSARY TOOLS

Knives could top my list of essential kitchen items, but then again, a couple of really good cooking pots are equally important. Cheap cook wear sets definitely aren't worth the money they cost and it's much better to have one or two decent pots as opposed to a matching set of not-so-good ones. Of this I'm certain. At least one of the

▲ Pot racks are great space savers that also come in handy for drying herbs.

large retail chains in this area has an amazing sale (50–75% off) on kitchen ware at least once a year and this is how I came to own a set of cookware that would normally be well out of my price range. And what a difference it makes. Several years later they're still just like new and I'm still just as crazy about them as I was the day I got them.

Maybe this is a good time to mention thrift stores, yard sales and online free-share sites because these are all places to find top quality gear at very affordable prices. I'm going to be mentioning the price of things a lot in this chapter because most of the people

I know simply can't afford to pay high prices for items they might need, or simply want, whether the price reflects the quality or not. I know there might be a few readers who might find such discussions to be boring and irrelevant. My apologies! For the rest of us, those of us with limited, or non-existent, expendable income, buying anything over and above our regular necessities creates its own set of challenges.

If my past life as a kitchen klutz enhanced my ability to write about developing kitchen skills, well, certainly my years as a single mom on a shoe-string income elevates me to near-expert status when it comes to making do with less. And yes, I know less is often more, but not necessarily when it comes to putting good food on the table. I'm going to be mentioning some fairly ubiquitous items and others that might have at one time seemed like unnecessary frills. Being someone who likes to keep things simple and who has always avoided extraneous gizmos like the plague, imagine my surprise when I discovered that some kitchen "stuff"—traditional and otherwise—really is useful.

I sometimes wonder, if I could only have one implement (in addition to a knife and a pot to cook in) which item would I choose, from the "adequate" selection of cooking tools I've managed to accumulate? Then I begin to think of all the people in the world who'd be delighted to own just one knife and one pot and I realize that the word "affluent" would be a better descriptive than adequate. It's all relative, and very much related to making sure the glass stays half full. That being said, here's my list, not of totally necessary kitchen aides, but of things that can be very useful in terms of saving both money and time.

Bowls

It is essential to have lots of bowls, including a couple of extra large ones and a couple of colanders. Nesting bowls are great because they take up less than half as much room, obviously. I was spoiled recently and given a lovely set of brightly colored Melamine bowls

(BPA free). Just love them, and I also have a set of stainless steel ones (I said I was spoilt) and yes, I use them all, especially around harvest time.

If mentioning the need for bowls seems insultingly obvious, the next item no doubt will also. Sorry! Having struggled for years without basic equipment, I know it happens and can taint the kitchen with a purgatorial ambiance.

Cutting boards

I have two big wooden boards, one which I keep for bread and pastry, the other for vegetables (in theory) and a couple of smaller boards which were actually one large cheap board that split in two. Even though it's nice to have a selection of boards, I wouldn't trade one big board for several smaller boards and once again, quality counts. The best way to clean a board is by wiping it with white vinegar and rinsing it under the tap.

A decent potato peeler—preferably one with a rubberized handle. Peeling vegetables is never a great idea as very often much of the nutritional content resides directly below the skin. The more that gets cut away, the greater the loss of vitamins and minerals. However, sometimes vegetables need to be peeled. I have seen a lot of people hacking away at various vegetable skins with a paring knife. So much waste that could be avoided!

A sturdy vegetable brush can, in most cases, avoid the need for peeling. My inner child insisted I buy one that looks like a large ladybug. Surprising enough, it's also highly efficient, especially considering that it only cost one dollar.

Bottle brushes are another of those very affordable purchases that can save a lot of time.

A limited selection of cooking utensils—tools such as stirring spoons and spatulas. I really favor bamboo for spoons but I find that plastic spatulas have a thinner edge and therefore perform better when working around the edge of a pancake or omelette. I think it is important to have a limited number of utensils, just the ones that are most commonly used. My list would read: two spatulas (one wide, one narrow), a ladle, at least two but preferably four bamboo spoons (two small, two larger), a large straining scoop, a slotted spoon and a flat edged, broad bamboo scraper.

Having too many utensils pretty much guarantees that you can never find the one you want (the one that's just perfect for the job on hand) when you need it. Lesser utensils such as salad servers, pastry brush, meat thermometer, carving fork and so on can stay in a drawer but the first group, those most regularly used, should be standing up in a ceramic container right next to the stove top, at the right hand side for those who are right handed and at the left side for lefties. I know that must sound so over the top, but the importance of a well-organized work space cannot be over emphasized. Bear with me. Remember, I'm the one who struggled through many years of not knowing this.

▲ A basic selection of good quality tools makes all the difference in the kitchen.

Spice cans

I tried keeping herbs and spices in a cupboard but that didn't work. The little jar I wanted always seemed to be the closest to the back of the cupboard. The dinky little sets of prepackaged spices are of limited value because while some might be useful, others might never even get opened. I find that small round tins (about two inches in diameter and one inch plus deep) with magnetized backs work really well attached to the side of the refrigerator. I can choose exactly what to fill them with and see at a glance which I need for the meal I'm cooking. Less used spices are stored in a basket at the back of a less accessible cupboard. Every kitchen has one! I write a list of all the spices in the basket so I can tell at a glance if I have what I'm looking for. Spices start to lose their efficacy after a year, even when tightly sealed, so it's best to buy in small amounts. Dried herbs that are homegrown can be replaced after each yearly harvest, that's if there's any left.

Oven mitts are so important! Definitely best to keep them hanging close to the stove so they can be grabbed quickly when needed. Trying to make do with a dishtowel is really silly because hot food can inflict nasty burns. A wet spot in a dish towel will transfer heat from pan to hand almost immediately and the instant reaction will be to let go. Oven mitts are relatively inexpensive, which is just as well because they have an uncanny ability to become scorched, stained and generally very grungy in a fairly short time. An oven mitt with half the stuffing falling out is even more dangerous than a wet towel. This is one of the rare instances when it pays to buy cheap and change often. And remember, you will need two. Even though gloves, much like socks and shoes, tend to come in pairs, oven mitts at discount stores tend to be sold singly. It's one of the great mysteries of the modern age.

A set of measuring cups, measuring spoons, at least one size of measuring jug (ovenproof glass with graduated measurements clearly marked up the side), an ovenproof casserole dish... It's beginning to feel like this short list could go on forever, not living up to its name at all. I think it's time to call a halt. Even though I know this is not a comprehensive list of all the items that will prove useful in the kitchen I'm hoping it's long enough to eliminate much of the seeming drudgery and the frustrations that are caused by not having the necessary equipment.

GIZMOS

Electric Wand Mixer

One appliance I came by as a gift was an electric wand mixer. I had thought one might be nice to have so I was quite pleased to receive it. The thing was I didn't have anywhere to put it because my kitchen is quite small, with not a lot of cupboard or counter space. Also, it came with a couple of interchangeable attachments which always seemed to be missing in action when needed and the handle, being

◄ These small, magnetized storage tins attached to the side of the fridge provide quick, easy access to most frequently used herbs and spices.

slightly top heavy, fell over whenever I tried to stand it up on the counter. These might sound like quite minor complaints but they were enough of a nuisance to obscure the usefulness of this little powerhouse. We had a "falling out" and the mixer was tucked away. For quite a while it never got used, mainly because I didn't have a dedicated and convenient space for it.

Eventually I wised up and reorganized the space, simply by finding a basket, perfectly sized to accommodate the wand and its attachments. I keep the basket in the cupboard right next to the stove where I can reach down and pull it out without even looking. That's convenience! Now that it is within easy reach I use it all the time for creaming soups and sauces, potatoes and squash and it blends salad dressing to perfection. It's just so much easier to clean than a blender and takes up almost no space, especially when compared to a full sized food processor that costs so much more, and takes three times longer (at least) to clean.

Salad Spinner

I know! I already mentioned a salad spinner in the chapter on greens, so I won't go on, much, only to repeat that they are very well worth having and keeping in a convenient place. They're quite large and take up a fair bit of space which makes a below the counter, bottom shelf a perfect spot. I'm sure most kitchens have a low shelf or cupboard where smaller items tend to get pushed to the back and forgotten about; out of sight, out of mind. This is the perfect space for the salad spinner. I don't have to get down on my knees to find it, I can just reach down and have it on the counter in a second. Certainly not rocket science, but I'm sure I'm not the only person whose head is usually full of ideas that are way more exciting than mundane stuff such as how to organize a kitchen efficiently. There are two basic types of spinner. One is activated by pulsating a knob on the lid, the other has a lever on the lid that is twitched forward and released. This is the type I am very happy with and I've been told it is preferable to the pump action design.

A Slow Cooker

I do need to come clean on this one because even though I have one, I almost never use it and could live quite happily without it. On the other hand I know there are many cooks who totally love and use their slow cooker several times a week, so I really feel obliged to mention them, but not as an experienced user. From what I can tell, they're brilliant for cooking meat and making stews, chili, soups and casseroles, and I would expect that they're beneficial in the sense that all the goodness and flavor of the food is maintained in the pot. I'm sure they're great for anyone who goes out to work and wants to come home to a good meal. Definitely, I can see that. I'm lucky enough to work at home and I almost never cook meat, so these may be the reasons I don't utilize the slow cooker as much as I might.

▲ A salad spinner and a "wand mixer"—two truly useful gizmos.

STOCKING THE PANTRY

Many food items which have an extended shelf-life are much more affordable when bought in larger quantities. Others that are seasonal, such as honey and maple syrup, might not be available for purchase year round. Both logic and logistics are involved here. First off, you might not have a "pantry"!

For me, a pantry is a space to accommodate dried or canned food that can be bought in bulk and stored effectively without refrigeration, such as rice and beans, nuts and dried fruits, cornmeal, sugar, oatmeal, tea… and so on. A pantry can be as simple as a couple of shelves in a designated cupboard or a small closet, or ideally, it might be a small room off the kitchen.

There are at least two very sound reasons to buy certain staples in bulk—one being food security, the other being economy. A small bag of rice for instance, costs way more per cup than rice bought in an eight kilogram sack. And the larger, less expensive amount will store almost indefinitely in large, recycled glass jars. Oils such as olive, safflower and canola are also much less costly per cup when bought in bulk.

Some canned foods, things that are regularly called for in recipes, such as canned milk, are best bought by the case. Of course the local food market is not going to cut any kind of a deal selling by the case but most areas have a bulk food outlet where discount prices encourage volume buying. Be warned, these can be dangerous places to enter! Some of the "deals" will seem too good to resist . . . and perhaps they are if you're serving five or six hundred people a week and are therefore likely to use a couple of kilograms of black peppercorns in a year. Otherwise, that's probably just too much pepper, no matter how good a deal it is.

The trick here is to decide what you will definitely use within a reasonable period of time. It's also important to weigh serving cost against initial outlay. If I'm only going to save a couple of cents per litre it might not be worth the strain on my food budget for me to invest in a six month's supply of soymilk. However, if I'm saving almost a dollar per litre on a product I use every day, well of course it makes sense. It's essential to be very clear headed about buying in bulk, and to promise yourself not to be "tricked" by a super discount price tag into buying a lifetime's supply of pineapple flavored hot sauce, especially if you don't really dig hot sauce.

A wisely stocked pantry eliminates the need for a weekly grocery shop, and perhaps more importantly, encourages a more creative approach to menu planning when meals are inspired by what's waiting to be harvested in the garden, augmented by what's available in the pantry. Perhaps the biggest plus is that time spent grocery shopping is freed up for more enjoyable activities.

TERMS & SKILLS—COOKING LIKE A PRO

I'm only including this next section to demystify what used to seem to me like a whole other world of words and references that I didn't understand. I'm absolutely not suggesting that they are here as instruction on how to cook. So why? Well, there are certain terms used in cooking that might seem a bit intimidating until they're more clearly understood. It's relatively important to know what they mean as many of them describe basic techniques which are simple enough and provide a useful toolkit when preparing any meal.

A roux for instance can transport a meal from bland and simple to exquisite and totally sublime. It was the basis of the sauce that transformed that freezer burnt salmon mentioned in Chapter Seven into a feast par excellence. Might sound fancy, but it's simply a mixture of flour, butter and milk.

How to Make a Roux

A roux is the basis of any white sauce, or gravy and is also the correct way to thicken soups, stews and chowders. The ingredients are very simple: Equal amounts of butter and flour plus a liquid for thinning, usually milk, cream, or in the case of gravy, vegetable water or stock. The process is a little tricky to master and, indeed, I know several highly competent cooks who prefer to substitute with a can of creamed soup such as asparagus or mushroom to thicken. However, learning how to make a roux really is worth the effort as it can make a totally inept chef look like something else. Believe me, I know. :)

Some Terminology

Sautéing or sweating? Steaming or braising? Soup or stew? What ever happened to boiling and frying? Well, they're still around but as food preparation gets elevated to its rightful status, fry ups and such are being forced to take a back seat. The differing terms indicate subtle but extremely important variations of technique and intended result.

Sautéing is to cook the food in hot butter or oil until it's browned and lightly cooked, thereby sealing in the juices and partially softening it. This effect is obtained by a cooking for a relatively short time in a small amount hot fat. With the food chopped into smallish pieces it can be tossed around in the pan to prevent sticking.

MAKING A ROUX
The butter, one quarter cup let's say (although any amount can be used as long as the ratios are kept the same) is melted slowly (that means over a low heat) and the flour (one quarter cup) is sprinkled over and mixed in with a wooden spoon to form a smooth paste that looks a lot like beige colored Play-Doh. Heat should stay around medium and stirring is constant. Here comes the tricky part—adding the liquid. Add it slowly and stir like crazy. As more liquid is added the risk of the dreaded "lumpies" lessens and the chef can relax while patting themselves on the back! They have just created their first perfect sauce which can now be flavored any way they choose. (And not to worry either way, you can always strain the lumps out.)

FRITTATA VERSUS QUICHE?
Is the real question, to crust or
not to crust? Well, yes and no.
I used to think it was the only
real difference between a quiche
and a frittata, but no, it goes way
beyond that. A frittata is actually more closely aligned to an
omelette and is in fact sometimes
referred to as an Italian omelette.
A frittata contains little or no milk
whereas a quiche has a custard
base, that is, a mixture of eggs,
usually two or three to about a
cup, or cup and a half, of milk
or cream.

The traditional way to cook
a quiche is in a slow oven (200–
250°F) in a well-greased shallow
dish, whereas a frittata is cooked
on the stove top in a skillet, in
much the same as an omelette,
but then quite often finished off
under the broiler.

The sky's the limit when it
comes to ingredients for either a
frittata or a quiche—the typical
ham and cheese or bacon and
tomato don't hardly scratch the
surface. A couple of my faves are
spinach and feta, or mushroom
and cauliflower, but any combination of your choices will work
equally well.

Sweating is also called "wilting," and is used to reduce the bulk of greens, such as spinach, without reducing them to a mushy mess. This process differs from sautéing as the oil can be replaced with a very small amount of water. The heat is considerably reduced and the cooking time is much shorter. The bulk in the greens will begin to reduce almost immediately and it's important to keep them turning so they keep the same consistency. Less is more here and the heat below the pan can probably be turned off after about a minute.

Steaming is a way of cooking vegetables and fish using the steam rising off boiling water. To do this properly the food needs to be elevated above, rather than submersed in, boiling water. The food is placed on a rack or in a vessel (such as a large sieve or steamer basket) which will allow the steam rising from the water to surround and cook the food, and which will fit inside a lidded cooking pot (containing a small amount of boiling water).

Poaching is usually done in a low oven, using a small amount of liquid such as stock, milk or melted butter that is served with the food (which is often fish) that it has been cooked in it. Eggs however are usually poached in water, on a stove top, over a low heat, in a covered pan.

Braising is much like poaching in that the cooking liquid is served with the food, often as gravy. The food is seared first over a high heat to seal in the juices and then cooked slowly in the oven with a liquid such as stock. This method works especially well on cuts of tough meat.

Soups versus Stews

Sometimes it's difficult to tell the difference and really, so long as it tastes delicious, who cares? Typically stews are a mixture of vegetables, including potatoes, with meat or fish, slow cooked in a small

▲ Crustless quiche? Or leek and tomato frittata? By either name this quick and easy dish is delicious!

amount of liquid and served in the cooking juice, which will have thickened up during the cooking process. Soups can have similar ingredients but tend to be less hearty and will be much thinner in consistency. Soup needs to be served in a bowl whereas stew is often served on a plate.

Frittatas versus Quiche

Who needs a quiche when you can have a frittata? Well, quiche used to be one of my faves and I quite liked making pastry until a couple of C words (calories and cholesterol) crept into my vocabulary. Almost overnight, cutting all the fat into all that flour was no longer a turn on, and pastry slid way down into the unhealthy food choice category. Frittata on the other hand…! Well, frittata is simply a quiche without the pastry—more or less.

Okay, so maybe that flaky piecrust surrounding the egg mix is nice once in a while, but frittatas take way less than half the time to prepare, have way less calories, and are certainly much healthier.

Pilaf versus Biryani

Another easy-peasey dish, or let's call it a concept, because really the parameters are so flexible it can be a starting point for anything you might want to make it, is a pilaf or biryani. And what's the difference between pilaf and biryani? Well, in my mind they're somewhat interchangeable. No doubt anyone who has grown up on the Indian continent will howl in disagreement at that. My apologies! Here's how the Oxford Dictionary describes them:

A pilaf is a Middle Eastern or Indian dish of rice (or sometimes wheat) cooked in stock with spices, typically having added meat or vegetables.

A biryani is an Indian dish made with highly seasoned rice and meat, fish, or vegetables.

They're both equally delicious, no matter what they're called! My favorite pilaf/biryani includes garlic and lots of spinach, kale or chard topped with some feta cheese and moistened with milk (or cream soup) and flavored with some crushed coriander.

Soups and Chowders

Soups are another ridiculously flexible dish. I mean really, just about anything can be made into a soup! Soups can be thick or thin, hot or cold. They can be very simple—one star and a small supporting cast, such as butternut squash soup—or they can have a gaggle of supporting actors, all with equal billing, such as in a typical vegetable soup.

A handful of barley, or a commercial "soup mix" consisting of various dried grains and legumes quickly transforms soup into a hearty, nutritious meal, or perhaps a single legume might be elevated to soup star status—black or white beans in a tomato based veggie soup for instance.

The base of any soup should be stock, either vegetable, meat or fish based. A stock is a flavorful liquid that is made by simmering bones, meat, fish or vegetables for an extended period and then straining and seasoning before use. I used to use only water so no wonder my soups always tasted, yes, watery! The easiest, although certainly not the healthiest, way to make stock is with commercially produced stock cubes. However, whenever I roast a chicken I simmer the carcass to make stock. If there is enough actual meat left on the bones it will become a chicken soup, but if they've been picked fairly clean it's more likely to become a vegetable soup, quite possibly "fridge soup."

And the difference between a chowder and a cream soup? Well "creamed" soups don't necessarily have cream (or milk) added but they are thickened and of a creamy texture, whereas chowders usually have a dairy base and the ingredients are usually fish or corn with potatoes and onions. I think of a creamed soup as something that has been blended, or creamed, whereas the ingredients in a chowder, though chopped, are still recognizable as "pieces of."

Casseroles

I might have thought that soups were an unwieldly topic but then I got to thinking about casseroles. Yikes! The term casserole can be applied to just about any savory one-dish meal that's cooked slowly in the oven. It's a bit like describing a group of people as movie goers. It doesn't help much to identify them individually, to describe their myriad personalities, just as the descriptive "casserole" does little to explore the enormous range of possible ingredients that can be included in any number of dishes that go by this name.

FRIDGE SOUP

Sometimes, food gets pushed to the back of the fridge and forgotten, no matter what the good intentions might have been. One way to reduce the risk of this happening is to make Fridge Soup a regular menu item. It'll always be different but with some good broth or a couple of vegetable cubes any combination of veggies can take on a whole new life. I used to think in terms of traditional vegetable soup, the typical mix of onions, carrots and celery, but actually just about anything can go in soup, and the addition of a little pasta or beans, along with a garnish of croutons and perhaps a generous sprinkle of cheese, makes magic happen! Scouring the fridge, the cold room and the garden once a week for anything that's looking a little weary and definitely like a potential soup ingredient is an excellent habit to get into.

The Take Away

While it's relatively useful to learn cooking terminology, it's perhaps more important to remember that this is nothing more than a labelling system for methods and while it's good to fully understand the rationale behind the methods, it's also important to remember that labels can be restrictive, not always conducive to creativity. It's much more exciting to let the ingredients themselves be the muse. A vegetable garden is a beautiful place, and I believe that nurturing the crops and watching them grow to maturity instills a better understanding of how they can be most perfectly prepared.

Off with the Gardening Gloves—
On with the Apron

It's time to make that giant leap into the kitchen! All that playing around in the garden has been rewarded by a bountiful harvest. Yikes! What to do with all this amazing food? There is one obvious answer to that, simply *eat it*, but it's so much more fitting to think in terms of creating something beautiful, at least as beautiful as the plants themselves, to celebrate the gift that they are.

Don't panic! I promise not to promote anything complex or time consuming. Beautiful vegetables are in themselves a work of art, so simply putting them on the plate is creating something special. It's rather like playing a game with brilliantly colored glass beads, arranging them into variously appealing patterns and combinations. It's fun, and the more you play the more skilled you become until there's no longer any need to refer to the rule (recipe) book—all the moves have been memorized and there's a growing confidence to be spontaneous and simply to enjoy.

Most of the "recipes" in this book are not really recipes at all in that they don't specify hard and fast measurements and lengthy lists of ingredients. I like to think of them more as suggestions with guidelines, frameworks which allow plenty of room for individual tastes and creativity.

◀ Crossing over the threshold— from garden to kitchen.

A Quick Recap—Important Elements

Let's start with color. Seeing as I'm talking about creating beautiful things, I think it's not too strange to begin here, even though nutrition should probably be the primary focus of any meal. Conveniently, the color of a vegetable often relates to its nutritional value. Two obvious examples are bright orange carrots with their high content of carotene and leafy greens such as kale, which are mega sources of vitamins and minerals.

I'm not sure where the phrase *eat your colors* originated but it was very quickly absorbed into the healthy eating vernacular because it's so appropriate. So, a multi-colored array of food is already having two very positive effects both sensory and nutritionally. The third crucial component to the meal has to be taste, with the sub-category, texture, because no matter how good a meal might look, if it doesn't taste great or if the texture is unacceptable, it's not going to be enjoyable and might not even get eaten.

In traditional Chinese culture it's considered bad manners not to want second helpings, as this is taken as an indication that the food is not so great. I've often thought that this could lead to difficult situations for people with very small appetites. I tend to gauge the success of a meal by the amount of food left on the plate. Never much and not often is what I aspire to. Does this sound like I'm talking in terms of dinner parties? No! This is about every day. Every day is special, we are special and we deserve the best. Simple as that. And yes, it is simple.

In the Garden—Potential Ingredients:

- Beets and greens, garlic and squash, beans and onions, leeks and potatoes, tomatoes and cucumbers.
- Parsley, summer savory, dill, cilantro, mint and chives.
- Rhubarb, Egyptian Onions, Sunchokes, Blackcurrants and chamomile.

  Looking at the list again I realize that the pairings must seem quite arbitrary especially as there are several other logical ways I

▲ Imagine! All this, on offer, every day of the week, at Mother Nature's country store (a.k.a. the garden).

could have arranged the chapters. I could have had all the Allium (onion) family members together, for instance, or the roots crop sharing several pages: beets with potatoes, beans with greens and so on. I believe I must have been wearing my chef's hat at the time, which had me thinking in terms of which veggies were just perfect together in some of my favorite meals, hence beets with greens (my fave salad), leeks with potatoes (my fave soup) and so on.

The fact is that the chapter groupings were immaterial because now all the veggies will be mixing and mingling like the best kitchen party ever. There are absolutely no rules that say they shouldn't! And if there were… well, you know what they say about rules, right?

9

Now We're Cookin'

with leeks & potatoes

WHERE TO BEGIN? Wow! There are just so many super simple, totally delicious combinations that I really don't know where to start. Let's imagine some potatoes, five or six medium sized (or maybe four large) and three or four leeks.

PREPARING LEEKS

I should give a warning here that the homegrown leeks might not be as big as the giant honkers usually seen in grocery stores. The top several inches of green leaf of any leek will be tough and need to be cut off. Some recipe books insist that all the green be removed and only the white part of the leek used but I don't agree with this. Over time it will become easy to know exactly where to make the cut but if you haven't prepared leeks before not to worry, an inch or two either way isn't going to make a huge difference.

Here's the important thing about preparing leeks: quite often small amounts of dirt will become wedged in between the leaf layers, just around the transition point where the leaves turn from green to white. I used to find this to be a real pain, enough in fact to deter me from wanting to use leeks. The problem was that I instinctively wanted to slice the leeks in the round, just as I do green onions. Wrong! The correct and easy way is to take the leek, nicely trimmed

▶ A fresh leek, sliced vertically and dunked a couple of times in clean water, easily releases any accumulated soil particles.

at both ends with all the ragged leaves removed and slice it lengthwise with the pointy tip of the knife, making sure to hold it firmly at the base so the leaves don't all come apart. This dissection reveals any dirt between the inner leaves, and there probably will be a little, especially in the outer layers. No problem. Still holding firmly onto the base of the leek simply dunk it up and down in a basin of water a few times. The individual leaves will fan out releasing all the trapped particles into the water. This is a very simple procedure that takes less than a minute.

Once leeks are cleaned in this way they can be sliced crosswise into half to one inch long pieces for soups and quiches or perhaps just cut into manageable lengths and lightly steamed or gently poached with butter for an elegant side dish.

Preparing leeks is not complicated and probably takes less time than it did to read about and definitely less time than it took to write about. It's one of those do it once and you can do it with your eyes closed actions (though not recommended, especially if the knife is sharp).

PREPARING POTATOES

Now, on to preparing potatoes. To peel or not to peel? Several factors come into play here, one being the type of potato. Some have coarse skins while other have delicate smooth skins—they definitely should not be peeled in my opinion. The thing is that much of the nutritional value, along with a lot of the flavor, resides in and just below the skin. When a potato is sliced in two it's often possibly to see a narrow line around the outer edge which is ever so slightly different in color. This, most all of the goodness of the potato, is what gets removed with the peel. Not good!

A really good scrub with a fairly coarse vegetable brush will make just about any potato perfectly edible, skin and all. However for those times when having the skin removed is preferable, definitely use a potato peeler, rather than a knife. I have watched people hacking away at spuds with a knife, effectively removing all the vitamins along with a goodly portion of the potato itself, and all because they believed they couldn't "get used to" using a tool specifically designed to do the job oh so much better. I can't help thinking that they must have had a really negative experience with a truly lousy potato peeler because no matter how slick you are with a knife, a decent potato peeler will do a far superior job, in half the time. More than enough said on that, especially as it is better not to peel in the first place!

MAKING A MEAL—WITH LEEKS & POTATOES

Let's just imagine four or five sparkling, lovely leeks. Really! There's something remarkably appealing about freshly cleaned leeks. When they're split down the middle, the delicate transition from green top to white base is revealed in the lemony yellow of the central core. Imagine also several chubby faced potatoes demanding to know their combined destiny. Well, hold on there, Spudleys! That's going to depend on a couple of things, available ingredients being one and intended purpose another.

I make a dish that I called potato leek strata, simply because it consists of layers, in this case potatoes, leeks, usually some cheese, perhaps some mushrooms and green onions. It's moistened with a little milk, with a couple of eggs whisked in to help it set up. For some reason I thought this dish was my own invention, so imagine my surprise when I discovered that there actually is just such a dish out there in the real world and not just in my kitchen. I think this goes to prove that a certain amount of food prep is instinctive.

A strata is not unlike scalloped potatoes, except much less runny. Whereas scalloped potatoes need to be served with a spoon, a potato strata is cut into squares and served with a spatula. Served with a colorful salad and perhaps a side order of pickled beets, those leeks and potatoes have been transformed into a perfectly balanced, totally delicious, home-grown meal.

CHEESE AND ONION SCALLOP
This is simply a layering of thinly sliced potatoes interspersed with sliced onions (or leeks) and topped with grated cheese. Milk (or cream), thickened with flour to a consistency of pancake mix, is then poured over the layers. The ingredients can be partially cooked on the stove top, prior to baking, especially if time is short, or placed directly into a greased casserole dish and baked at 350°F until they pass the fork test (prongs should slide in easily), about ninety minutes max.

POTATO LEEK SOUP

Simmer several potatoes, peeled and roughly chopped into bite sized cubes, in just enough water or stock to cover. When almost tender add two or three similarly prepared leeks and continue to simmer until both are tender. Season, and add milk which has been thickened (see How to Make a Roux in Chapter Eight) and blend lightly.

POTATO LEEK SOUP

Everyone has their own special comfort food and I'm thinking that mine might just be potato leek soup. I'm dreaming of it even as I'm seeding the leeks in the very early (and usually very chilly) spring, long before the potatoes are even in the ground; but it's not until the clocks have been set back and the winter wood is well stacked and already in use, that leek and potato soup tops the menu, served with homemade bread and spicy croutons, of course.

DRESSING UP POTATOES

If potatoes have jackets, I like to think of gnocchi as potatoes in tuxedos. They have a certain gourmet mystique about them even though in truth the most difficult thing about them is learning exactly how to pronounce their name. I'm still not sure! I suspect they're actually the Italian cousins of pierogies, several times removed... or are pierogies some distant Polish relative of gnocchi?... but then I read somewhere that the Chinese *were making pierogies when Europeans were still barking at each other* (not my words!). So totally irrelevant, I know, but I just thought it was fun to learn how the origins of food can be fiercely contested, and also that boiled, then fried, potato concoctions have been eaten for a very long time.

Even so, I still find that they tend to be somewhat heavy in texture and most often rather bland in taste. (Gasps of indignation here, along with the assertion that this is only because I have never tasted mother's, or grandmother's, wondrous gnocchi, pierogies, or dumplings.) Enough already!

Irish Mashed

Sometimes, a main course or a family member cries out for simply mashed potatoes. But why would anyone want straight mash when they could have Irish mashed potatoes or better still Colcannon. Unfortunately, most Irish mashed potato recipes require oodles of butter and cream (Colcannon always also includes some chopped cabbage) and are not likely to be found in any heart or hip friendly recipe collection. However, cottage cheese makes a very palatable substitute for much of the no-no stuff and anyway, to my mind the most important addition is garlic, and secondly chopped green onion or chives—behold, the humble potato turned rock star!

Rumbledethumps!

If the Irish Colcannon has a distinctively pleasing lilt to it, what does the name of the British concoction of left over potatoes and cabbage convey? Bubble and Squeak, as I am assured, refers to the noise of the cabbage and potato hitting the hot fat in the fry pan. Really! It'll take more than that to convince me that it doesn't, in fact, refer to the gastrointestinal confusion of a digestive system trying to deal with what just came down the pipes. Rumbledethumps is the equally apt Scottish name for this potato cabbage fry up.

Enough frivolity, back to the text!

Leftovers?

The best thing about mashed potatoes can indeed be the leftovers. Fish cakes anyone? Or potato pancakes or chive parsley patties? Or as a topping for some shepherd's pie or vegetable casserole? The possibilities are endless.

Bakies and Wedges

Another way to prepare potatoes, and perhaps one of the more efficient ways from a nutritional standpoint, is to simply bake them. Just scrub them, prick them with a fork, oil the skins and pop them in the oven. A medium potato will take about an hour at 350 degrees. Serve with butter, sour cream, grated cheese and chives, green onions, bacon bits or any or all of the above, and they are almost a meal in themselves. My choice would be to add a crunchy salad, but then a salad completes just about any meal in my book.

In a hurry? Potatoes cook much, much quicker (in about 30–40 minutes) when cut lengthwise into wedges, with the skins still on, before oiling. I usually quarter and then half each of those quarters

GNOCCHI

Gnocchi is fun to make but beware—it can become the comfort food of choice! Not many ingredients here, simply potatoes, flour and an egg, plus cheese and seasoning to taste—I like to add chopped parsley. Two large potatoes, boiled and mashed, are mixed with a cup of flour and an egg to form a stiff dough. The dough is rolled into snakes, sliced and rounded into bite sized pieces which can be, but don't need to be, ridged by pressing gently with a fork. These are plunged into boiling water and left until they begin to rise to the surface, indicating that they're done and can be removed using a slotted spoon. Most recipes seem to end here but I have learned, from where or whom I don't remember, to then brown them by sautéing in hot butter. The choice is yours, depending on how many extra calories you want to rack up. :)

▲ Herbed "wedgies" with chipotle sour cream and a crunchy salad. Yum!

so I end up with eight wedges from a medium to large potato. I then toss them in a bowl with some oil and dried herbs. Rosemary is my special favorite but an Italian garden mix is nice for a change, and of course they can be spiced up with some dried, crushed chilies and chopped garlic. It's fun to experiment and potatoes are very amenable to this!

Let's all praise the humble potato indeed! I could go on but the not so humble leeks are demanding equal billing.

LOVING LEEKS

Leeks are the elegant aunt of the Allium family, having a flavor that is refined, yet distinct enough to be recognised as part of the onion family. They are brilliant in quiche, especially when paired with feta, and they're equally wonderful in stir fries, contributing their own unique color and flavor to the mix. Braised in a little veggie stock then topped with a little butter and a couple of twists of fresh pepper, they are nothing short of decadent.

Nutritionally leeks are quite similar to garlic, if slightly less potent. They contain flavonoids and other antioxidants, minerals and vitamins and, as with garlic, various compounds which convert to allicin when crushed. Allicin is particularly valuable as it reduces cholesterol formation and helps keep blood vessels flexible, thereby reducing the risk of stroke and coronary disease. Leeks are also a good source of vitamins such as niacin, riboflavin, thiamin, folic acid and pyridoxine, as well as A, C, K, and E.

Leeks (and also daffodils) are the national emblem of Wales and yes, because I am half Welsh I might be ever so slightly biased, but doesn't it speak volumes to the nature of the leek, that it would be chosen to represent a country? Of course I have heard the reverse hypothesis, suggesting that it doesn't say much for a country that it would pick an onion as its iconic representative. To this I only have two words. Not funny!

Joking aside, I've always found it a bit confusing that the daffodil is also used as the national emblem, especially since they don't seem particularly interchangeable with leeks in the garden and, as daffodil bulbs are highly toxic, they certainly have no place in the kitchen either. Here's the why: *Cenhinen* is the Welsh word for leek, *Cenhinen Pedr* (St. Peter's leek) is the word for daffodil, and over the centuries it seems that which choice was the original pick became unclear. My vote definitely goes to the leek, as Saint David, the patron saint of Wales, ordered his army to wear leeks in their helmets in a battle against the Saxons, which was fought in a field of, yes, you guessed it, a field of leeks. Now that I've clarified that point… I have also no doubt left some readers wondering "Do I really need to know all that?" just to make leek and potato soup? Well no, I just thought it was rather interesting. :)

POTATO PANCAKES

These brilliant little pancakes start out much like gnocchi but with less flour, in this case I add a tablespoon of flour to each cup of cooked, mashed potato, along with chopped green onions (and/or parsley) and grated cheese to taste. The mix is rolled into palm-sized balls and flattened to form patties about one half inch thick which are then floured and then fried until golden and crispy.

The addition of some flaked fish will transform these into fish cakes, which are usually rolled or "breaded" in corn meal before frying. Even something as simple as a can of salmon will transform left over mashed potato into the mainstay of a meal; add a salad and everyone's happy!

10

Super Salads & Beautiful Beets

I'M WRITING THIS CHAPTER just around the time my spring salad greens are sprouting up in profusion. It's so wonderful to be able to start the day by wandering around the garden while everything is still cool and often still shining with the previous night's dew. I call this my early morning slug patrol but it's more accurately my pre-breakfast foraging foray because I can't resist nibbling on a couple of young kale leaves here, some arugula there, and some mâche and some Tat Soi and so on.

Greens eaten this way bear little resemblance to anything that is being sold pre-packaged in the stores, and truly, just one of these "foraging" trips makes all the hard work preparing the soil worth every aching muscle. Without a doubt this is the best way to eat salad greens—no plate required! However, I can't quite imagine inviting friends over for supper and then taking them into the garden and telling them to tuck in, so yes, summer greens sometimes need to be served on a plate and yes, they can be almost as delectable when served at the table.

HARVESTING GREENS—A REMINDER

I did mention the importance of correctly harvesting greens in Chapter Three but I will recap because there are a couple of very simple but equally essential elements to keep in mind. Primarily, the "field heat" phenomenon. Field heat will cause the freshest, crispiest of greens to wilt beyond recognition within an hour or so, which is why it must be neutralized ASAP. This is easily done by plunging the greens into icy cold water as soon as they're picked. The escaping heat can actually be felt rising from the greens. Also, a short soak and a gentle swish around will rinse away any flecks of dirt and insect grubs, which will all sink to the bottom of the dish pan or bowl, leaving the greens ready for a quick twirl in the salad spinner prior to serving or bagging and storing in the fridge for later use.

Also, it's best to pick greens in the morning before the more intense heat of the day, but after the dew has had chance to evaporate. It's never a good idea to work in a wet garden because simply brushing against damp leaves can help to cause/spread fungal diseases.

▲ Just a few of the enticing herbs, oils and vinegars available for salad dressings.

DRESSING SALADS

The early salad leaves are more delicate in texture and to my mind lend themselves to a light vinaigrette as opposed to a heavier, cream style dressing. Not that early greens need anything to enhance their taste—they really don't. Sometimes though, it's nice to "party" them up a bit. It probably comes as no surprise that homemade dressings are really far superior to commercially manufactured dressing and very much healthier and more economical. For the longest time I didn't even attempt to make my own dressings. I guess I had it in my head that to do so required unobtainable ingredients and some alchemystic training. Not so. Just the opposite in fact. The basis of most dressings tends to be simply oil and vinegar with the addition of various herbs or spices, depending on taste.

Oils

I guess it could be any kind of oil or vinegar but I would not use a basic cooking oil such as corn or canola oil unless I had nothing else and was absolutely, totally stuck for some oil. It's heavy and not the healthiest. Even though the oil in a dressing is virtually invisible it can have a huge influence on the nutritional benefits as well as the

> **SIMPLEST DRESSING EVER**
> The best ever kale salad dressing in my opinion consists quite simply of lemon juice, mayo/sour cream and maple syrup…remembering that most of the oil was already added when massaging the kale leaves (Chapter Three).

HERBED VINEGARS

Herbed vinegars are the easiest things to make: simply chop a half a cup or so of fresh herbs into a bowl and cover with heated vinegar. Cool, cover and let stand for four or five days, then strain and pour into a sterilized jar or bottle, and finish off with a sprig of fresh herb. Tarragon, basil and chives are favorites for herbed vinegars.

taste of the dressing. There are many wonderful oils available, such as avocado, safflower, olive and various nut based oils, which do cost more at the cash register—but how does that compare against the impact of ingesting oils from genetically modified monocrops such as corn and canola? Before I go off on a rant about industrialized farming I'd better get back to light summer salad dressings!

Vinegars

I'm similarly a bit particular (or is that peculiar?) about vinegars. I tend to think of white vinegar as a chemical. Do I want to ingest something I clean the drains with? Nah! I much prefer to use apple cider vinegar—especially as it's often referenced for its health promoting qualities. It's said to be very good for the digestive system and also for relief of pain from arthritis. There are several other types of vinegar that are lovely for dressings including rice wine vinegar, red wine vinegar and, best of all, herbed vinegars, which are very easy to prepare at home. Perhaps my favorite vinegar after apple cider is balsamic but I tend to shy away from it as a dressing for early salads because its dark brown color will detract from the glorious melange of vibrant greens.

Juices

Fruit juices can be a perfect third ingredient for light dressings and even though I'm referring to the apparent "physical weight" of the dressings here, a juice based dressing will have far less calories than one that's heavier on oil. Orange, cranberry or mixed berry juices all work wonderfully well and eliminate much, if not all, need for any sweetener. Lemon juice can be used instead of vinegar and indeed, perhaps it gives the dressing a fresh tanginess, but too much can be harsh and I usually add extra sweetener when using lemon juice. Of course fresh squeezed lemon juice is by far the best but I don't have a lemon tree growing in my kitchen so I like to keep the bottled version in my fridge.

Sweeteners

I used to always use honey to sweeten but recently I heard an interview with an apiarist who suggested that, in light of the current crisis in the bee population, we should stop taking honey so much for granted, and should think of it more as a treasured medicinal rather than as an everyday sweetener. His thought was that if bees were allowed to keep more of their precious winter store that they'd labored all summer for, perhaps they'd stand a better chance of rebuilding their population. I'm not sure how that would work from an economic perspective but, even so, I've switched to maple syrup as my sweetener of choice and have read that it is in fact more nutritious than honey. The review I read was written by a syrup producer, so could it have been a tad biased? Perhaps, but since they are friends of mine I'm choosing to believe it. :)

It's important to note that real maple syrup, used as a sweetener, will not impart that somewhat sickly, overbearing "maple" flavor that pervades donuts and other "maple flavored" products. I suspect that the closest they come to any tree product is the paper they're served in. (Oops! Did I just say that out loud?) Real maple syrup does, in fact, impart a very delicate sweetness and, in my opinion, first greens deserve a delicate dressing to complement their personality. So, when I say sweetener, I actually use maple syrup. However, understanding that it can be pricey and not always available, I want to make it clear that just about any sweetener can be substituted: honey, stevia, demerara sugar, and even plain white sugar, which would be at the bottom of my list. Corn syrup is not even on the list as it is exceedingly unhealthy for a host of reasons.

So, the basics for any dressing are oil, vinegar (or lemon juice) and sweetener. This basic mix can then be adjusted and enhanced in any number of ways by the addition of various herbs, such as fresh garlic or dill and spices, hopefully gathered straight from the garden.

▲ A warm chard/beet salad topped with toasted walnuts and feta cheese.

Creamy Dressings

As the summer progresses and the greens mature, the structure of their leaves becomes stronger, more able to support heavier, creamier dressings. In my mind a basic creamy dressing is similar to a vinaigrette with the addition of a mayo type substance to thicken it up and make it opaque. Gasps of indignation here from the "gastros," but please remember, I'm the girl who likes to keep things simple, having no pretensions towards gourmet whatsoever. But I do know what tastes delicious!

Mayo works well but it can be replaced with Greek style yoghurt, sour cream or even avocado, all much healthier alternatives and probably better tasting. If none of these are available it's easy to thicken milk up by adding a little lemon juice. I find this especially useful if I've made a creamy dressing that's a bit runnier than I'd like or if I have neither yoghurt nor sour cream in the fridge.

A berry juice added to a creamy dressing will give a pleasant pinkish tinge whereas balsamic vinegar will turn the dressing a deep mushroom color. I didn't find this color appealing when I first encountered it in a restaurant (partly because it reminded me of a donkey I once had an altercation with) but the taste won me over immediately and on darker leaves such as kale, spinach, chard and beet greens, the color is barely noticeable.

Delicious as a balsamic dressing is on kale, nothing, but nothing, beats a simple lemon/mayo/maple dressing (see side bar). Some things are just meant to be together and to my taste this is one of those combinations. When making dressings, feel free to

BASIC SALAD DRESSINGS

I never actually measure the ingredients for salad dressings or for much else come to that. I like to think this is a more creative way to approach things. (Many might disagree!) I usually start with a base of the main three: oil, vinegar, sweetener, and then go from there, with at least one other ingredient.

Thinking in measures of tablespoons a typical recipe might read,

2 Tbsp of oil, 1–2 Tbsp vinegar, 1 Tbsp of real maple syrup.

Then I might add some grainy mustard to taste starting with 1 Tbsp or some prepared cranberry sauce (I will probably reduce or even eliminate the maple syrup in this case). Or perhaps I'll go with some peanut butter for a nutty flavor. The finger test works best here for me and as long as it's a different finger for each taster... well, this still won't satisfy food safety regulations, so I really should advise using a series of clean teaspoons for tasting!

The vinegar I use is never plain white, but usually apple cider or balsamic. Balsamic is not as "tart" as other vinegars so it requires a little less sweetener and its richer, fuller flavor is lovely in dressings. Lemon juice can replace vinegar altogether but it can be a tad harsh, especially if it's bottled rather than fresh squeezed, so it's better to start with just one Tbsp and work from there. It's much easier to add a little extra but impossible to subtract once it's already mixed.

A small jar (4 oz./125 ml) is perfect for shaking the ingredients together but I've learned the hard way that it's very important to make sure that the lid is tightly screwed on!

▲ Crispy homegrown greens really don't need any help—but it is fun to dress them up once in a while.

get creative! Remember, it's all about taste, your particular taste, so add, subtract and adjust amounts until the dressing tastes perfect... to you.

Other Salad Ingredients

Up until now I've been focussing on the leaves in a salad but in fact I seldom serve just leaves. The word salad refers to a mix of ingredients and the possibilities are truly cornucopian. The creative potential in the simple act of making a salad is close to infinite and depends primarily on what's available in the garden and in the pantry, but over time it also becomes heavily dependent on personal preference. I really like fruit and nuts in my salad and, as I'm sure has become perfectly obvious by now, I'm heavily influenced by color. What's really cool, when what's in the garden dictates what goes on the plate, is that meals transition, creating a gentle ebb and flow as crops ripen and then set back.

Salads are a yearlong staple in this house but the nature of the salads varies greatly from one month to another. Even so, some of the ingredients are regular, some 365 day a year visitors to my salad bowl are apples, dried cranberries, nuts, seeds, grated carrots and grated beets, all things that are readily available year round from the pantry or the cold room.

Of course the very best way to get a child interesting in eating fresh veggies is to encourage them to grow their own in a specially designated garden. It doesn't need to be a big space, a big planter will do at a pinch, but a name tag and a fun touch such a friendly gnome (and really, doesn't every garden need to have one?) works wonders.

Salad with Protein

If I'm serving the salad as the main course I like to add an additional protein source, such as cheese, either cubed, crumbled or flaked; or perhaps some sliced hardboiled or pickled eggs. When I have an eggsess I hard boil and pickle some eggs for just this purpose because I seldom plan ahead to allow time enough to hard boil, peel and slice eggs for a specific meal. Having a couple of jars ready and waiting in the fridge suits my kind of time management so much better. Nuts and seeds are another tasty way to add protein to a salad. I keep a jar of mixed nuts and seeds on the counter so I can throw a handful on top of the salad in a second. Healthy eating is just that easy.

Croutons

Homemade croutons also give substance to a salad, especially when it's being served as the main course. And again, they are so easy to prepare that it's hard to understand why they would be offered for sale commercially, even before a taste comparison. Really! It's little wonder that croutons aren't mainstream popular if that's how they're offered to the public—boxed croutons bear so little resemblance to the real thing.

Once again, they're not something to be made right at supper time. Much easier to make ahead, especially when there's some homemade bread about to go stale and an oven already warm from baking something else. I like to keep a jar of these crunchy little bread bites on the counter, and judging by the way they have a habit of disappearing, even when I haven't been sprinkling them on soups and salads, I suspect they make a tasty little snack food all by themselves. It goes without saying that home baked bread indisputably makes the best croutons. The good news is that the hardest thing about making croutons is keeping the home baked bread around long enough to turn it into croutons!

There could be, well, I'm sure there are, books dedicated to nothing but salads because the possibilities are limited only by the ingredients on hand, our own imaginations and of course by the ultimate test—taste! This last factor is subjective, but only to a certain degree. Much as I like strawberries and sardines, the thought of them in a salad together doesn't do a thing for me, but who knows, perhaps there's a mom-to-be somewhere who might find such a salad quite delightful. But now I'm getting silly! Time to move on to beets.

SWEET/SOUR APPLES

An important note here about using apples—definitely no need to peel, but after they've been cored and cubed they should be sprinkled with a little lemon juice and then tossed in a little sugar (about the only time I use white sugar). The lemon prevents the chopped apple from turning brown and the sugar provides a sweet/sour surprise. I suspect that the addition of foods that (I hope) most kids are familiar with as snacking treats, such as apples, cranberries, carrots, etc., will help attract them to salads, which can be a bit of a hard sell if they have not yet identified with their inner bunny.

CROUTONS are crispy, flavorful bread bites that are often sprinkled on salads (especially Caesar salad).

Simply cut bread into bite sized squares (they certainly don't have to be exact), sprinkle with olive oil and toss in a large bowl with fresh or dried herbs and possibly some finely chopped garlic. They can be cooked in a skillet on top of the stove but this requires diligent supervision and a very big skillet! I usually tend to burn them this way and prefer to use the oven. How hot of an oven? There seems to be a variety of opinions on this. I prefer a hot oven for a short time because I think the bread is less likely to dry out and become too hard when it's toasted quickly. However, I usually try to use the heat from something that's already in the oven, so I've discovered there's lots of flex room regarding temperature.

BEAUTIFUL BEETS

Having already mentioned the nutritional qualities of beets I won't go there again, only to say that eating beets is being very kind to your body and your body will thank you! I did also mention this next point in Chapter Three but it's so important I think it can stand repeating. Whatever method is used to prepare beets, the skin is not cut or removed until after the beet has been cooked so as to avoid loss of nutrients and taste. This also makes life easier as the skin slides off a cooked beet, easey peasey. (This applies to most root crops but to a lesser degree.)

Preparing Beets

The skin on the top of the beet, surrounding the tuft where the leaf stalks were trimmed off, is usually a bit rough and flaky and it's natural to want to cut this away but no, a stiff vegetable brush will remove any grit that's lodged in around this area while leaving all the nutrients still safely contained under the skin. It might seem counter intuitive not to cut beets, especially the larger ones, in half at least and especially when boiling, in order to reduce cooking time, but instead, if boiled beets are required, remove any smaller ones as they become tender and allow the larger ones to remain in the water for longer. This really is better than cutting and watching all the juices leach out into the water.

Roasting Beets

However, when roasting large beets, perhaps it is better to half or quarter them but still with the skin intact. They will have been brushed with oil prior to roasting and this will help seal the juices in. The skin will slide easily off the roast beets after they're cooked. I guess it's a bit like wrapping a potato in foil before cooking, which makes me think that beets are probably delicious wrapped and roasted on the barbeque. I haven't tried this yet, but I think I will.

I realize there was some contradictory information floating around there. Cut beets/don't ever cut beets? To clarify, try to avoid

▲ Beets are just plain beautiful! Also highly nutritious and super versatile.

cutting beets prior to cooking, don't ever cut beets before boiling and try to avoid doing so when steaming. With roasting it becomes a compromise because the longer the beet is roasted, the more the nutritional content is diminished. Anything over an hour is well onto the downhill slide. So, probably better to quarter large beets to ensure shorter cooking time. I think I nailed that one! But no! All the previous statements fly out the window when it comes to making beetroot curry.

Beetroot Curry

For this popular Sri Lankan dish the raw beets are peeled and cubed then simmered in the curry sauce until tender. I'm okay with this because my theory is that even though the nutrients will seep out of the beets themselves they will still be contained in the sauce and in the rice the curry is served on. Oh so good! Just thinking about it makes me want to stop writing and make this curry.

Making Curries

And while on the topic of making curries: making them from scratch can be expensive. Even though curry recipes vary immensely they all require a variety of spices; black mustard seed, turmeric, garlic, coriander, cayenne pepper, bay leaf and cinnamon, just to name a few. Only two of these are growing in my garden. My initial cost to purchase all the other spices would be around thirty dollars and when I add the cost of a few additional ingredients I could easily be looking at forty dollars. Yikes! I'd need to sell tickets to that first curry dinner. I find it much easier, and definitely a smaller initial investment, to buy curry paste (another gasp from the gastros). Yes, it's sort of cheating I suppose, but I like to keep things real... real simple that is.

Having said that, I have met people who just love to make curries from scratch. Curries are their "signature" piece and it's truly lovely to sit in anticipation, hearing the spices sizzling as they hit the hot oil and smelling the bursts of spicy aroma. I would never dissuade anyone from aspiring to make curry from scratch. It's just not for me. For me, a jar of curry paste and can of coconut milk work quite fine, thank you. :) Yes, coconut milk! Be warned, it's loaded with calories, and it's not inexpensive, but it can redeem a lackluster curry with the simple twist of a can opener.

Raw Beets and Lebanese Pickle

I've talked a lot about cooking beets but they can also be eaten raw, grated into a salad or a slaw, and I'm sure this is the very healthiest way to eat them. Certainly an amazing flash of color sprinkled on a green salad. I'm going to finish this section on beets by raving yet again about their color. Echoes from Chapter Three! Anyone who has enjoyed Lebanese food and especially falafels will doubtless be familiar with pickled turnip, that wonderfully tangy, brilliantly pink addition. The main ingredient is just a plain old turnip but the true maestro of that mix is the beet. Would that pickle be as appealing (or even palatable) served "undressed," nakedly white and beetlessly forlorn? I don't think so!

11

Garlic & Onions, Squash & Beans

THIS CHAPTER HAS shades of a family party with its combinations of cousins and sisters and deep seated antipathies. The cousins—garlic and onions—are both members of the Allium family. Squash and beans, though not from the same family, are two of the sisters in the revered Three Sisters planting schema. In the garden, onions and beans definitely do not get along, but in the kitchen (and in this chapter) they have promised to play nice.

SQUASH

As already mentioned there are two types of squash, summer and winter, and their differences become quite apparent in the kitchen. The flesh of a summer squash, such as a zucchini or a yellow neck, is more porous and moist than the flesh of a winter squash, which is much denser. The skin of a winter squash is tough enough to protect its flesh for several months of storage, whereas a young zucchini has a much thinner, more tender skin. This skin will harden up if the zuke is left overly long on the vine, but generally will not get as hard as the skin of a winter squash.

Cooking Squash

The skin on a summer squash is perfectly edible and I prefer to leave it in place, even when cubing or slicing for salads or stir-fry. It's really a good habit to think that any scraping or peeling is removing nutrients along with the skin, but of course, in some cases, the skin just has to go. Winter squash is a perfect example of this.

Removing the skin from a winter squash is not easy and definitely requires a very sharp knife or a cleaver. It's actually much easier to roast the squash with the skin on and then scrape the flesh off the skin. I suspect this is also the best way to conserve its nutritional integrity. Prior to baking, the halved or quartered squash is seasoned, dabbed with butter or brushed with oil, and it can be sprinkled with a little cinnamon and even some brown sugar if you're feeling particularly decadent.

I have to admit that, more often than not, I peel winter squash before baking, but that's just me. For some obscure (and as yet unidentified) reason I find that scraping the flesh off the skin doesn't feel right instinctively, even though intellectually it makes perfect sense. Go figure!

GINGER SQUASH SOUP

The basic requirements for a squash soup are 2 onions, at least two cloves of garlic and of course an acorn or a butternut squash, along with several cups of chicken or vegetable stock (or two or three stock cubes), a little butter and some seasoning.

I like to add the zest, juice and pulp of at least one orange (I often add two) or perhaps a handful of chopped dried apricots or sometimes an apple. None of these are essential but they do add an interesting dynamic to the flavor. I also add grated ginger (remember to peel it first Jenni or you'll get all the stringy bits in the soup!) and possibly a little canned milk. Naturally, curried squash soup will require some curry paste or powder. (Truth is, squash soup always tastes good, no matter what goes into it.)

Method

The onion (chopped) along with the garlic and ginger are gently cooked in the butter. If I'm wanting a curried soup I will add a tablespoon full or so of curry paste or powder when the onions are translucent and almost cooked.

The more common method is to bake the squash and then scrape off the skin but I prefer to remove the squash skin first and chop the flesh into pieces, a bit too big to be called bite-sized. When the onion garlic mix is cooked, I add the squash, cover well with several cups of stock and simmer slowly, covered. When the squash is well cooked the mix will be very thick and will probably need diluting with more stock and perhaps a little canned milk or coffee cream before it is blended (using the handy, dandy wand mixer mentioned in Chapter Eight) and served with parsley, sour cream and croutons.

▲ Baked zucchini filled with a feta/ rice/almond mix, spiced with garlic scapes and served with a kale salad.

I don't ever boil or steam squash because it will turn bland and watery, but be warned, chunks of Butternut or Acorn squash that have been tossed in oil and lightly seasoned before baking are totally irresistible when they come out of the oven! One taste tends to lead to several and suddenly the squash is almost gone before it's even reached the plate!

Yes, such is my love of squash—so, no surprise that squash soup is another favorite of mine. This is where garlic and onions jump into the mix, along with an apple and probably some fresh ginger or curry paste. I also like some feta cheese crumbled on my soup with a sprinkle of fresh parsley to provide the perfect contrast against the deep rich yellow of the soup. To me this is perfection, but I can also live quite happily with a dollop of plain yoghurt and a sprinkle of paprika.

Stuffed Squash

Winter squash, and more mature summer squash, can also be stuffed or "filled." The term filled used to confuse me (this is embarrassing) because I couldn't figure out how I was supposed to get the stuffing inside the squash. If this isn't perfect proof of what a kitchen klutz I was, well then my secret is safe. Forever!

Obviously the squash needs to be sliced or halved prior to filling, a step I had failed to visualize in my confusion about how one might go about stuffing a squash. It's then scraped clean of seed and pith which leaves a nice little cavity for the filling. The flesh is oiled and baked covered at 350°F (175°C) for approximately forty minutes, then for a further fifteen minutes uncovered. These times vary according to the type and size of the squash being roasted. A summer squash, such as a large zucchini or a vegetable marrow will need less time because their flesh is much less firm and has a higher water content. I start testing for readiness by piercing with a fork after about thirty minutes. The squash should not be mushy but soft enough to allow the fork to slide in easily.

If the squash is intended as a simple accompaniment to the meal, prior to baking it might well be seasoned with cinnamon, a sprinkle of nutmeg, a dash of sugar... But just baking with a rub of oil is equally fine, especially when the squash is destined to be stuffed.

And with what? This is the wonderful thing—I can't think of much that wouldn't go well with squash. This broadens the potential for creating amazing meals exponentially! In terms of a well-balanced meal there will be a carbohydrate, such as rice or quinoa, and a protein such as beans, nuts, cheese or meat, and a vegetable or fruit for color and additional nutrition. Tomatoes, parsley, spinach, raisins, mushrooms, pine nuts, sweet corn, apples, celery, peppers, melon... the list could go on and on. The great thing is that with different fillings, this meal never ever gets boring and when it's served with a fresh green salad the color combo makes it look almost too beautiful to eat. But not to worry, the aroma quickly discredits any notion that this feast is primarily a visual delight. It's massively delicious and so easily adapted to personal preferences and the ingredients on hand. Just to clarify, the stuffing is usually prepared (cooked) on the stove top before it is introduced to the squash, so it doesn't take more than twenty to thirty minutes in a medium heat oven for the flavors to meld together perfectly. Baked, stuffed squash is a win, win, win!

Double Baked Squash

One last word on baking squash... and just when it might have seemed that there was nothing left to say... the double, or twice baked squash. This simply means that after the squash is baked the flesh is scraped out leaving just enough in place to keep the skin rigid. The flesh that is removed is then pureed with addition ingredients such as cream cheese, chopped chives, mayo and seasoning then returned to the squash skins, topped with breadcrumbs and baked for a further 15–20 minutes. It's much the same process as stuffing or "double baking" potatoes, except that to stuff a potato it's totally necessary to scoop out the innards in order to create a cavity for the filling. With squash, a cavity already exists waiting to be filled so, in my opinion, the double baked recipes seem to create a lot of extra work for no particular purpose, other than to use the flesh of the squash as the major ingredient of the filling. Doesn't this seem like a bit of a redundancy?

GARLIC & ONIONS

Meanwhile, back at the party, the cousins, garlic and onions, are hanging out in one corner grousing about how they're never fully appreciated, how they're sick and tired of always being seen as secondary ingredients. And yes, they do have a point. Without them, where would soups and stews, sauces and stir-fries be? At the Boring baseline is where, along with oh so many other meals that might have thought they didn't rely on garlic and onions for their success when, in fact, they do! So many do that it might be easier to list meals that would not benefit from the addition of an onion or a clove of garlic, rather than try to name all those that do benefit. Yes, garlic and onions deserve better, so here are, especially for the Alliums... drum roll... French Onion Soup and the power-packed variation, Garlic Soup.

FRENCH ONION SOUP

The Easy Way

The base of French Onion soup is beef broth but vegetable broth can be substituted. If beef broth is to be used the easiest thing (by far) is to purchase cans of beef broth or consommé, the difference being that broth is thinner and less flavorful than consommé. Not sure which to use? Either/or works, and it really depends on personal preference. A good plan might be to mix them, using a can or two of each, for starters and then go from there. Beef cubes will also provide a perfectly useable broth. I usually use veggie cubes and color the liquid up a bit with soy sauce and a dash or two of Worcestershire Sauce.

Method

Two or three onions along with at least a couple of cloves of garlic are browned in butter then simmered in the stock for five to ten minutes. When done this mixture is divided equally into little ramekin bowls (over-sized cups will work, just as long as they're oven proof) and topped with lightly toasted bread. French bread is the traditional choice but any bread will be fine, as will croutons. The bread is then covered with grated cheese—Gruyère is perfect but mozzarella will do and the cheese is then toasted under the grill until bubbly and slightly browned. Be sure to give the soup a minute or two or three to cool off slightly!

French Onion Soup

While neither of these soups *need* their own special set of bowls or ramekins there is something "souper" special about individual portions, each with its "lid" of crusty bread topped with sizzling cheese, usually Gruyère, Swiss or mozzarella. The origins of onion soup date back to Roman times when it was considered to be a poor man's meal because onions were plentiful and easy to grow, but the modern day version originated in France in the 1700's.

Garlic Soup

Last winter when it seemed that we were besieged, with pernicious flu bugs about to attack from all sides, I made some onion soup but substituted about a third to half of the onion with garlic. Might sound silly but not only did this soup taste amazing, it really worked and we remained healthy despite all odds. This could not be a year round innovation because come spring whatever garlic, if any, is left over from the previous fall's harvest will be starting to sprout and turn soft. By then it's no longer of much use in the kitchen and can be stuck in the ground as a very late planting. (Keeping in mind that garlic should actually be planted in the fall.) Conveniently, by this time the worst of the flu season is hopefully over, and the need for such an intense immune system boost is lessened.

However, there is a traditional garlic soup that uses considerably less garlic and certainly deserves a mention for its excellent taste and nutritional qualities, and for the fact that it is a brilliant way to use stale bread. This soup is claimed by a variety of countries and there are French, Spanish, Italian, Czech and Slovakian versions, the main differences being whether the garlic is roasted first or simply crushed and heated in oil. As usual I opt for the simplest way, which is to crush the garlic, then cook slowly in oil before adding cubed bread, vegetable stock and finally a couple of lightly whisked eggs. After a slow simmer for twenty minutes or so the soup is blended (again with the handy dandy wand mixer mentioned in Chapter Eight) and is served as a creamy, garlicky, intensely satisfying, brilliantly nutritious meal in a bowl. Mustn't forget the parsley garnish (I like to be generous with my garnish) and perhaps a final sprinkle of paprika.

Onion versus Garlic Soup

Despite the seeming similarity of ingredients, there are a several basic differences between the traditional onion and the traditional garlic soup. Onion soup is meant to be brown so the onions are caramelized, and of course the beef stock is brown, whereas garlic soup is meant to be pale, taking on the color of the bread and chicken stock, so the garlic is not browned. Garlic soup is thick because the bread is blended in whereas onion soup is thin with the bread as a top crust. Garlic soup has a couple of eggs added whereas onion soup has cheese as an added protein. It's interesting how many quite radical differences there are between these two soups which might have been expected to be more or less the same.

I realize that I've spent quite a while discussing these two soups and this because I consider them to be essential additions to any long-term menu plan. They're quick and easy to prepare, as well as being very inexpensive and highly nutritious, but perhaps even more importantly, they're intensely satisfying in the cold of winter and give our immune systems an added boost when most needed.

Caramelized Onions

Onions are not much for standing alone and they don't generally pop up as the star performer of a meal. They're not particularly sexy either but they can be the final touch that transforms a meal when they're "caramelized." I have to pick my words carefully here because in truth I'm just not that crazy about caramelized onions. This might very well be because I've never cooked them exactly right and therefore don't really know what they're supposed to taste like! I tend to rush the process and end up with onions that are reminiscent of my early days in the kitchen—with a blackened mess rather than delicately browned crispies.

People "in the know" rave about caramelized onions, so it's only fair to mention this method of preparing onions. Full sized onions, not green or Egyptian onions are required for this method. The onion is first skinned then sliced in half from top to root end, placed flat side down on the board and sliced, still in a lengthwise direction, to form strips about one quarter inch wide. These strips are then slowly, gently browned in skillet with some oil. Occasionally they will need to be stirred and towards the end of the cooking process they will begin to stick to the bottom of the pan but a small amount of balsamic vinegar will fix this. The caramelization releases the sugars in the onions which gives them a particularly sweet, oniony taste. Once well browned and crispy, the onions are cooled and stored in a jar in the fridge to be used as a tasty topping for burgers and many other dishes. It's probably more than just a good idea to prepare a batch ahead of time as this is a process that can't be rushed. They don't need constant attention while they're cooking but they do need about thirty minutes over a low to medium burner with occasional stirring.

Other Ways to Cook Onions

Fried onions start out in a similar way but the cooking time is considerably faster and shorter, usually just until the onion slices turn translucent and ideally become slightly browned along the edges. Onions can also be baked, in their skins on a baking sheet or peeled, quartered or sliced thickly and topped with dabs of butter in a casserole dish. When baked in this way the resulting liquid can be turned into a creamy sauce and of course the nutrient loss is negligible when the cooking liquid is served along with the vegetables.

NB boiling, that is, prolonged cooking while submerged in water, is actually the worst way to cook any vegetable, and can be easily avoided by braising, steaming, baking or sautéing.

At the moment, the only things I can think of that won't benefit from the addition of some garlic or onions are apple pie and porridge.

▲ A super delicious veggie casserole topped with some turkey sausage.

Just kidding! I'm sure there are a few other meals that don't need any help from the Allium cousins. The cousins, in turn are quite happy to hang out alone once in a while, simply roasted or braised, and served as a side.

BEANS

When it comes to beans, well surely there must be books written about nothing but beans. They offer such a huge range of versatility and variety, but generally speaking, or so it seems to me, these qualities are highly under-appreciated, along with their nutritional value. I know they have inspired a couple of rhymes, but we won't go there!

Baked Beans

As a child, the only baked beans I was familiar with came in a can and were served on toast. Beans on toast was a regular item on a lunch time menu. When I first came to Canada I was puzzled by the elevated status baked beans seemed to enjoy, with various acquaintances claiming that their mother's, or their granny's, baked beans had to be the best ever.

Well! When I got to sample some of these marvellous home-baked beans I was not impressed. In fact I didn't like them one bit and still don't. I found them stodgy, verging on indigestible and way too sweet. 'Nough said. It wasn't until a friend who had spent years living in the South of France introduced me to cassoulet that I realized that beans do have enormous potential.

Cassoulet

Traditional cassoulet is loaded with fatty meats such as duck, pork, mutton and sausage. However, there are many vegetarian versions which replace the meat with a selection of fresh vegetables, along with the staple ingredients, white beans, tomatoes and herbs, topped with breadcrumbs and slow baked. I'm sure any French chef worth their salt would throw up their hands at such a travesty, and in truth, it might be more accurate to call this a "veggie bean casserole," considering that half the traditional ingredients have been removed, but cassoulet sounds so much tastier.

Variety and Versatility

Black, white, red, pinto, garbanzo, kidney… the number of types of beans available is equalled by the global range of gastronomic variations. Mexican refried, spicy Moroccan, East Indian dahl are just a few bean dishes that instantly come to mind but I'm sure there are hundreds more delicious ways to prepare beans, each representative of their particular point of origin. Along with their extreme versatility, beans are inexpensive, super easy to store and perhaps most importantly, when combined with rice they supply a "complete protein." A complete protein contains all nine of the essential amino acids that our bodies need but are unable to produce themselves. However, this certainly does not mean that beans must always be served with rice.

▲ A well-stocked pantry is nothing less than a blessing.

As a final super plus, beans can be sprouted mid-winter (or any other time for that matter) to provide sprouts for crispy, crunchy salads and sandwich toppings. In my kitchen I'm still barely scratching the surface on the potential for beans and probably always will be. I'm sure that all over the world there are small communities known for their particular speciality bean dish. Sometimes I think it would be fun to gather bean recipes considered to be most representative of all the various countries and regions, but then I wonder, would canned beans swimming in tomato sauce be chosen to represent Britain? Yikes! They wouldn't hardly stack up against a perfect cassoulet from the south of France, or refried spicy blackbean fajitas from Mexico, now would they? I know, I'm not being at all fair to my country of origin and besides, there are a lot worse things than a plate of beans on toast, I think.

Preparing Dried Beans

For any bean recipe (when starting from scratch, that is, using dried beans) it's necessary to soak the beans overnight in plenty of water,

3–4 cups for each cup of beans. The soak water is then discarded, the beans are rinsed and well covered with fresh water, brought to the boil and then simmered until tender. The cooking water should not be salted as this will turn the beans squishy. The cooking time will vary immensely depending on the type of bean, anything from 30 minutes to two hours and more. It's important to rinse all dried beans thoroughly before using as typically they go straight from the field to the package and can pick up a goodly amount of dust and grit along the way. There is also a "hot soak" method which simply means that the beans are brought to a boil in the soak water for five to ten minutes and then left to soak overnight. This method will reduce the cooking time somewhat.

Either soaking process can be a bit of a challenge for those of us who aren't great (or are hopeless) at planning ahead and don't usually know what's going to be on the supper menu until it's time to start preparing it! Fortunately there is another, much less time consuming way to incorporate beans and this is to use canned ones. There's a wide selection of commercially canned beans, readily available and reasonably priced. I like to have several cans in the pantry so they're ready for use the moment I decide that they're what I need for supper.

I know that encouraging the use of commercially processed food must seem contrary to the main purpose of this book, which is to empower readers to revel in the food they've grown themselves. And I suppose in a way it is, but the way I see it, those dried beans in the pantry, the ones we've grown and dried ourselves, they're like an ace in the hole, a guarantee that there will be nutritious foodstuffs to coast through on should conventional food sources fail, or become inaccessible, for whatever reason. Also, a lot of home grown veggies will be accompanying those canned beans. I tend to favor canned black, white and red beans and of course I'm referring to the actual pulse, the seed of the bean, and certainly not the limp, tasteless whole "green beans" that come in a can. Green beans have to be fresh or fresh frozen from my own garden. Or they just don't make it to the table.

Lentils

Just a note: Technically lentils are a grain rather than a bean and are probably better loosely connected with dried peas rather than dried beans. There are three types of lentils: spilt or red lentils, green lentils and brown lentils. But why? Well the red cook the fastest at twenty minutes or so, whereas brown, which are still encased in their outer skin, are much slower cooking at about forty-five minutes, and they also have the strongest flavor, which compliments heartier dishes such as spicy lentil soup. The green lentils take about thirty minutes to cook, hold their shape much better than the red ones, and have a pleasing taste which makes them an excellent addition to salads, once they're cooked, of course. I usually cook lentils from scratch as they don't require overnight soaking and don't take too long to cook.

Peas

Goober peas are actually peanuts, which are in fact a legume rather than a nut, and are part of the bean and pea family. Unlike peas, they like it hot and dry, so unfortunately we have not yet been able to grow them on our damp, often chilly island. Optimistically, we keep trying because they are a solid staple crop.

But for now, we have to remain happy with fresh green peas, not so hard to do, especially when they're picked in a summer garden and eaten right there on the spot. Yummeee! If there are any left by the time I reach the house, they will be perfect slivered in a salad.

I much prefer the edible pod strains of peas, even when they're not for instantaneous consumption. They're also perfect when picked young and lightly sautéed, either with slivers of red pepper or in a stir-fry. The actual pea in an edible pod isn't noted for its size, and indeed, by the time the peas have swollen to typical pea size

SPICY LENTIL SOUP

First off simmer a cup to a cup and a half of brown lentils in five cups of veggie stock for an hour or so. While the lentils are cooking, sauté a couple of chopped onions with at least two cloves of garlic (three may be better). A teaspoon of chili powder sparks this soup right up, but it's not essential and depends totally on personal taste. Add the onion mix to the lentils along with one and one half cans of chopped tomatoes to start (you might need the other half can, depending on consistency). Finally add three or four cups of fresh (or frozen if necessary) kale, spinach or chard, along with some chopped parsley, and serve. This makes for a nutrient rich mega meal!

PEAS

"Peas, peas, peas, peas!
Peas, peas, peas, peas!
Goodness how delicious
Eating goober peas"

Just imagine I'm singing that…
but on second thoughts, perhaps
not. Better I leave the singing
to Burl Ives, Johnny Cash and
several other greats who have all
recorded their own versions! This
traditional American folk song
originated during the last years
of the American Civil War when
the Confederate Army was cut
off from food supplies and boiled
peanuts were often the only food
available.

the pods are likely to have become tough and stringy. The key is to pick these peas young and often, but remember—never when the leaves are damp as this will proliferate the various fungal diseases that pea vines are susceptible to. Fresh young peas are an early summer crop and once the vines start to look dry and weary it's time to remove them.

Frozen peas do seem to maintain a lot of their fresh picked quality and are one of the very few processed vegetables I use. A handful of frozen young peas sprinkled in a curry add such a perfect counterpoint to the dense earth tones of a typical curry, and the little sparks of bright green seem to almost vibrate along with the red of sweet peppers and the brilliant orange of carrots and sweet potato. And of course they add a similar visual pizazz to biryanis and chowders.

Even the regular (non-edible pod) pea varieties are harvested relatively early. If left too long and the fall comes wet and way too early, the peas are likely to turn moldy on the vine. Pod peas left too long on the vine also tend to taste pasty and they certainly lose any pleasant sweetness they might have had. Dried peas = soup in this house. I prefer the green to the yellow because…? Well, that's just me and my color preferences. Whenever I dry peas they are pretty bland looking so the actual color of my soup is usually dictated by whether the peas have been home dried or purchased.

Mushy Peas

No section on peas would be complete if it didn't mention mushy peas. These are the peas served with fish and chips and to anyone who hasn't strolled along on a typically damp English night, eating fish and chips with a side order of mushy peas, all wrapped in newspaper, I have to say, *That's really too bad.* :(Just for the uninitiated, I will explain: mushy peas are dried marrowfat peas that have been soaked overnight in water with some baking soda added, drained and then boiled up with a pinch of salt and a pinch of sugar. The soda causes the peas to sort of "explode" and become a mushy green mess.

▲ Perfect! Peas so sweet they seldom make it as far as the kitchen.

If that doesn't make them sound very appetizing, well I'm sorry, it's the best I can do. A typical British "chippie" will have a vat of them slow simmering all day, perhaps to ensure that any resemblance to the vegetable these peas started as is long gone. Mushy peas—once tried never forgotten!

12

Cukes & Tomatoes

THE SPEED AT which I'm whisked back in time by the smell of fresh tomatoes is really quite dizzying! It's like I have a lifetime, intercontinental travel pass—disguised as a nose—that never fails to transport me back to my three year old self (chubby legs and all) standing in the doorway of my uncle's ramshackle greenhouse (I was never allowed beyond this point) simply inhaling the spicy, exotic smell of tomatoes. It's really curious how powerfully those moments imprinted on my psyche.

Not that tomatoes are my hands down, all-time favorites, even though such a fruit, newly ripened and picked straight off the vine, takes some beating for sweet, juicy flavor. The range of varieties available is truly amazing and some, especially the cherry types, are remarkably sweet.

COOKING TOMATOES

To my way of thinking all fresh tomatoes are better left uncooked but here's the rub, lycopene, the highly beneficial phytochemical present in tomatoes, becomes even more accessible when the tomato is cooked. It doesn't take much and over-cooking is a cruel thing to do to a fresh tomato. It does nothing to improve their flavor while effectively destroying their pleasantly firm texture ... a quick sautéing in hot oil with a little salt and pepper and perhaps a sprinkle or two of fresh chopped basil, now that's another story. Simple, yet delicious!

Of course, come frost time, if the harvest of red tomatoes is massive, canning tomato sauce is probably the way to go. In truth I've never had much luck with this, primarily because plum tomatoes make the best sauce for the same reasons that I don't plant them, because they aren't the best for eating fresh off the vine, having less juice and pulpy flesh.

When a typical globe type tomato is cut, a naturally occurring enzyme immediately sets to work separating the juice from the flesh. This process is deactivated by heat but this has to be a fairly immediate intervention, which is why canning recipes usually recommend preparing one jar at a time. Yikes! That sounds like slow progress to me. My other problem is that if any other vegetables, such as peppers or mushrooms, are added to the sauce it must be processed in a pressure canner. These are expensive and I find them quite scary, but that's another story.

GREEN TOMATOES

I've been dreaming on about a plethora of luscious red globes but the boney finger of reality keeps tapping me on the shoulder in time to a harsh chant—Green tomatoes! Green tomatoes!

What to say about them? Well, fried up they make a good movie. :) It's a very long time since I watched *Fried Green Tomatoes* but, as I recall, the plot revolved around a restaurant that served the best fried green tomatoes. I tried to make them, but only once! To be fair I'd never eaten them before, properly prepared or otherwise, had no idea what they were supposed to taste like, and any cooking tips the movie might have offered, other than embedded in the title, were pretty much non-existent! Since then I've found a bit more information on this southern favorite. It requires a heavily seasoned corn meal batter to coat the slices of tomato, and these are then deep fried until crispy.

BIRTHDAY TOMATOES

My dear husband made me a wonderful supper for my birthday. It included the best tomato salad I've ever tasted. Very simple but oh so tasty—cherry tomatoes, halved with chopped green onions and some pine nuts and arugula (could substitute cilantro or parsley for arugula), all soaked in a mix of olive oil with a generous spoonful of oyster sauce. This would be the perfect boost for tomatoes that might have become a little lackluster.

GREEN TOMATO MINCEMEAT

Just like Momma
Used to Make

12 C chopped green tomatoes
6 C green apple chopped
2 C raisins
1 C currants
1 C candied citron peel
3 C brown sugar
2 tsp cinnamon
¼ tsp allspice
1 tsp salt
¾ C vinegar
¼ C lemon juice

Method

Simmer all ingredients together in a big pot (a very big pot) until tender, about one hour. The mixture is then transferred into sterilized jars and processed for twenty minutes in a water bath.

The green tomato recipe of choice around these parts, especially among the older generation, seems to be chow. Personally I just don't like it, not one bit, so I'm going to set it off to one side along with the home baked beans with pork scraps and molasses. Sorry, but I can't be nice about green tomato chow. This is totally subjective. My bad!

Green Tomato Mincemeat

Green tomato mincemeat, well, that's something else. It might sound less than tempting but my mom used to make it and my family loved it. Her mince pies were vacuumed up the minute they touched the plate. It's much lighter, less cloyingly sweet than regular mincemeat, so definitely an improvement in my book.

Ripening Tomatoes

Surely the best thing to do with green tomatoes is to ripen them up. This is best done in brown paper bags in a cool dark place but certainly not in the fridge. The success rate won't be one hundred per cent and a lot will depend on how far the tomato has progressed through its growth cycle while still on the vine. However, it's nice to extend the "fresh" tomato season, and it can be by a considerable amount of time. One year I had a massive amount of green cherry tomatoes still on the vine at frost time, and was able to keep them ripening up through to December. The original taste was much diminished but no more than with commercial grade tomatoes.

CUCUMBERS

Cucumbers, much like tomatoes, are surely best eaten raw. I like to score the outer skin lengthwise with a fork before slicing. I remember hearing years ago that this helped release any excess acid, but I just do it because it makes for an attractive, scalloped edge. Another way is to remove strips of the skin with a peeler or a sharp knife, creating a striped effect. This helps to modulate the flavor of the cucumber without removing most of the nutrients which reside in the skin and seeds of the cuke. While still on the topic of cucumber skin it's worth

▲ Green tomato mincemeat! Might sound strange but it tastes delicious.

noting that *cucumbers that have not been homegrown might well be coated with wax*. All the skin should be removed in this case, unless you plan on auditioning for Madame Tussaud.

Raita

Cucumber pairs well with dill or mint and can be served sliced in apple cider vinegar, sour cream or plain yoghurt. Raita is an East Indian dish which is simply cucumber, peeled and thinly sliced or

▲ A homegrown Greek salad—quick and easy, nutritious and truly delicious!

chopped, in yoghurt with mint or cilantro leaves. (Interestingly, in most of the Indian recipes the chopped leaves are referred to as coriander, rather than cilantro.) Raita is very refreshing, especially with hot spicy dishes, and it's super simple to make, but it is important to remove as much moisture from the prepared cucumber as possible by pressing it gently between sheets of paper towel or a clean dishtowel. Otherwise the raita will quickly become watery. Using the thicker, Greek style yoghurt also helps to avoid this.

Greek and Other Salads

Cucumbers, along with tomatoes, are two of the main ingredients in Greek salad and they go equally well in a host of other salads that might include beans, grains, corn, fruits and seafood. They're very versatile and seem to complement most summer meals, cucumbers being particularly compatible with seafood such as shrimp and salmon. Dill with cucumber is the perfect marriage!

PSEUDO GREEK SALAD

I call this a "Pseudo" Greek Salad because I think technically a true Greek salad uses sliced red onion, and a non-sweetened oil/vinegar dressing with lots of oregano. Typically I tend to find this a little harsh in taste. I prefer to use green onions and a sweeter dressing, and fresh cilantro. I've also been known to add some homemade corn relish or some canned corn, which I'm pretty certain breaks the rules but certainly adds a beautiful yellow sparkle to the other colors, along with the added sweet corn flavor.

2 C cherry tomatoes, halved

1 lg. or 2 sm. cucumbers, partially skinned and cubed

1 C chopped green onion (or red onion if preferred)

½ C cilantro (and/or parsley) coarsely chopped

1 C black olives, pitted and sliced

1 C feta cheese cubed

1 C corn relish or corn niblets (optional)

Dressing

¼ C olive oil

¼ apple cider vinegar

2–3 Tbsp maple syrup

1 tsp prepared sweet mustard (optional)

1 tsp oregano or to taste

Salt and pepper to taste

Combine in jar and shake

13

Herbs
a magical mystery tour

HERBS ARE THE small but mighty final touch that can be subtle enough to be almost indistinguishable, or they might be the flavor that jumps in and drives the bus—which might be fine, or could just mean that extra spoonful was a BIG mistake!

It's important to remember that taste is highly subjective and that most herbs speak directly to our taste buds. Parsley is one of these in that it doesn't shout out to my olfactory senses, not one bit, but I love its fresh, slightly peppery taste and, of course, its brilliant green colour. Summer Savory on the other hand is quite insignificant in appearance, with small greyish green leaves and even smaller flowers, but man, those leaves have a pungent aroma and are not particularly pleasant to simply "graze" on fresh, the way I like to do with parsley.

Herbs, perhaps even more than other plants, have very diverse, but prominent personalities. If they were to assume "ladies of a certain age" personalities, parsley would be dressed in something flowing and colorful, with lots of clunky jewelry, bright red lipstick and she'd have a contagious laugh.

Summer Savory on the other hand would be sitting ramrod straight in greys and a well pressed blouse. She'd also be a world traveller with a dry wit and multiple humanitarian credits, but it would take a while to fully appreciate who she really was.

There is something rather mystical about herbs and they have a way of becoming an intrinsic part of the summer routine, almost like they're part of the family. Perhaps that's why I tend to relate to them in terms of human personality. Or perhaps I'm just a little strange. :)

Years ago, but fewer than I'd care to admit, any discussion of herbs left me cold. I just didn't understand what all the fuss was about, didn't cook with them, and certainly wasn't interested in growing them. I have no idea how my relationship with herbs changed so radically, but I'm ever so glad it did because they're really quite interesting and very beautiful, each with their own understated elegance.

As already mentioned in the chapter on growing herbs (Chapter Seven), they possess a myriad of curative and restorative properties. I have a couple of beautifully illustrated herbals that I was fortunate enough to pick up in used bookstores. They give the historical background of each herb, along with its botanical and medicinal profiles, as well as its culinary uses. Much of this information dates back hundreds, if not thousands, of years and traces links or threads that connect to the distant knowledge of our ancestors. We might now have scientific analyses and oodles of formal education but I believe our ancestors understood on a much deeper level how to connect with the earth. Working with herbs makes me think I'm somehow reconnecting with some of this lost knowledge.

Enough with the magical mystery tour! Now I'm wondering if I've been way too pragmatic in my choice of herbs mentioned here. But no, ratcheting myself back to that time when herbs were a complete non-entity to me, and realizing that this opinion is probably more common than not, I guess the four or five basic herbs chosen are as good a pick as any. They're all quite well known and commonly used except perhaps for cilantro/coriander, but that's okay too as it will hopefully help to open the door on the endless world of possibilities that herbs offer.

PARSLEY

I've already mentioned the amazing nutritional benefits of parsley in Chapter Seven and certainly these qualities are reason enough to really use parsley, to consider it not as an occasional frill but more as an essential, in much the same way many cooks think of salt. The notion that parsley is best left untouched at the side of the plate needs to be attached to some large heavy object and dropped down an abandoned mineshaft! Seriously though, parsley is way more than just a garnish.

If it's being added to cooked food this should be done at the end of the cooking process to preserve maximum colour and nutritional benefits. Having a large pot of parsley growing right outside the kitchen door is a major step to elevating parsley to its rightful status.

Parsley is usually chopped when added to soups, sauces, egg dishes, etc., but a handful of the leaves simply stripped off their main stems are lovely in a mixed salad. In a predominantly parsley salad such as tabbouleh, however, it's usually coarsely chopped.

Some dishes require that herbs be more finely chopped. Garlic bread, for instance, is sprinkled with finely chopped parsley after

TABOLEH One Great Way to Stay Healthy

This Middle Eastern dish is another of those salads that contains all the major food groups and serves them up in the best way possible. The main stars are parsley, bulgur and tomatoes but it welcomes other ingredients such as chick peas and cucumber and it's flexible enough that it doesn't mind substitution. For example, couscous can replace bulgur. What's the difference between them? Well, bulgur is an ancient form of whole grain made from crushed, partially boiled and then dried wheat. Couscous is very similar. It is made from semolina wheat which is hulled and crushed, but not ground, then sprayed with salted water to help it cluster into tiny pasta beads. Traditionally, couscous is always steamed and *never* boiled. However, typical North American recipes tend to suggest simmering or steeping in boiling water.

1 cup of bulgur (or couscous) is simmered for about ten minutes in one and three quarter cups of water and put to cool while chopping two tomatoes, one cup of cucumber, a cup of parsley, half a cup of green onions and one quarter cup of mint. One can of chick peas, drained, can also be added but these remain whole.

All the ingredients are mixed together with a dressing that consists of lemon juice—one quarter cup, olive oil—a couple of table-spoons, a couple of finely chopped garlic cloves and salt and pepper to taste.

▲ Parsley—a true powerhouse of nutrition that will spark up any dish with its fresh, peppery flavor.

it has been spread with garlic butter. This is when it really helps to have a really good knife (or cleaver) and a decent cutting board that isn't warped and wobbly.

CHOPPING HERBS

Firstly, the parsley is rinsed and shaken to remove any excess water and then the leaves are shredded from the main stem, which might be a little too coarse to leave in the mix. I leave the finer stems attached but some might prefer to remove all the stems. When chopping a very large amount of parsley it might be easier to use the chopping attachment that usually comes with a typical wand mixer, or a blender but it's awfully easy to over process and I much prefer to chop by hand. I'm used to chopping with a knife and it really doesn't take long, not at all, once the technique is understood. If I need to chop a large amount, I don't try to chop it all at once because it's much easier to go with two or three smaller amounts—a good handful at one time is plenty.

A chef's knife, this is the big wide one that tapers quite sharply to a point, works best. Some people, my husband included, prefer to use a cleaver but the process is much the same. After a few rudimentary chops to flatten the pile, the forward tip of the knife is held down on the board so that the chopping action is actually more of a rocking motion. As the knife edge rocks up and down it also pivoting from its point from side to side over the parsley. This will cause the leaves to spread out, so every so often the knife is used to scrape the semi-chopped parsley back together for further chopping. This is a quick, simple operation that very soon becomes second nature. I like to chop more parsley than I think I'll need so that I can keep a small bowl of it already prepared on the counter. It will stay fresh for several days but will probably have been used before that.

▲ Bundles of herbs can be hung just about anywhere to dry.

PRESERVING

Parsley doesn't dry well and it's much better to mix it with a bit of softened butter and freeze it, divided into portions in an ice cube tray. Summer savory on the other hand is best dried. Herbs really should be hung in a cool, dark place to dry but I just love to have bunches of herbs hanging to dry in the kitchen. I have a big pot hanger over the counter and it's just so convenient to be able to reach up a grab the herbs I need. Of course, it wouldn't be good to leave the herbs hanging up there indefinitely. Once fully dried they are best stored in airtight containers in order to better maintain their potency.

SUMMER SAVORY

Once summer savory has been dried, it's very easy to remove the small leaves from the woody stems by simply holding them over a bowl and running the hands down the stems. Summer savory is usually "rubbed," that is, massaged briskly between the palms and fingertips to release the tiny stems which might still be attached to the leaves and to break up the leaves, which, when dry, are quite brittle. Most of these tiny stems can be removed by shaking the dried savory through a coarse sieve, but a few always seem to slip through.

No biggy! The more obvious ones can be removed immediately prior to use, if this seems necessary. Personally I think they give a rustic authenticity to the meal. If this really doesn't appeal another option is to grind the herb to a much finer consistency.

CILANTRO/CORIANDER

What to say about cilantro? Sometimes I love it, sometimes I think I don't like it very much at all, so I'm somewhat stuck for words on this one. This love/hate relationship all began a couple of years ago when my neighbour Jennifer made a delicious dish that relied heavily on cilantro. It was truly delectable, enough so that it inspired me to pledge everlasting allegiance to the taste and to plant masses of cilantro the next year. The next year came, along with waving fields of cilantro (perhaps a slight exaggeration here) but unfortunately neither Jennifer nor I could remember the name or nature of that oh so delectable dish she'd prepared the year before. I'm leaning towards a phyllo pastry or a cheesy, polenta type of dish... but then again, was it not a fresh relish with cranberries and walnuts? Obviously I really have no idea what it was that initially convinced me that yes, indeed, I do love cilantro. I do! I do?

And then there's coriander, the seed of cilantro (see Chapter Seven). Equally strong and distinctive in flavor, it's typically more prevalent in East Indian and Asian cuisine. Sometimes I find myself wondering whether I grow cilantro/coriander simply for its quirky, split personality, but I never have any such doubts about my reasons for growing dill.

DILL

Dill! The leaves, the flowers, the seeds—they're all so very fresh tasting and nothing sings summer quite like fresh dill... well, except for fresh strawberries and a few other things like that. I refer to dill "leaves" but the leaves are actually very delicate, feathery fronds with a wonderful scent and a delicious taste. As the dill matures, the main stem these fronds are attached to becomes quite woody and inedible.

I only chop dill coarsely, if at all, and especially love it added directly to salads of just about any kind, to salad dressing and to sauces. Salmon, poached, fried or cooked on the grill without a generous rub of dill, well that's just criminal! The flowers make the loveliest edible garnish and the seeds are super easy to save. Nothing says home grown and made with love better than a full seed head tucked into a jar of dill pickles. It's beautiful when growing, just as attractive as any flower in the garden, wonderful in a vase, amazing to taste, fresh or frozen, either as dill butter or as flavor cubes (frozen as separate portions in ice cube trays, then bagged). Dill is one hundred per cent worth planting.

MINT

I like mint best when dried and then steeped as a tea. Fresh, it's quite lovely sprinkled in with new peas and tiny new potatoes. It pairs well with cucumber, is also interchangeable with parsley in many salads and it makes the perfect garnish for ice cream, as it leaves the palate feeling fresh and clean. It does, however, seem to be a taste that is either loved or hated. I really like it but because I'm the only one in this household who does, I restrict my use of it.

I hate to admit, but I have never even tasted mint julep. The fact that William Faulkner, Scott Fitzgerald and even Charles Dickens had lots to say about it makes me think it must indeed be quite special. Apparently, the exact nature of the epitomic julep was a hot topic among quintessential Southern gentlemen, and the ability to make one was most decidedly a required social grace.

I thought this quote by Frederick Marryat was quite fun. (Marryat was a British naval officer and a novelist who popularized the genre of the "sea story" and also developed a system of marine signal flags in the early eighteen hundreds.) According to Marryat: "They say that you may always know the grave of a Virginian as, from the quantity of julep he has drunk, mint invariably springs up where he has been buried."

DILL PICKLES

Dill pickles have to be a close contender for the easiest pickles to make, ever!

Sterilize four jars (see Chapter Fifteen) while boiling together two cups of white vinegar, two cups of water, and two tablespoons of pickling salt.

Pack several small cucumbers, along with a head of dill and one peeled garlic clove into each jar and pour in the boiling liquid to one half inch below the rim. Cover and process in a water bath. Ten minutes for one pint jars and fifteen minutes for one quart jars.

How simple is that!

◀ Even after their feathery leaves have been stripped off and used in the kitchen the exquisite dill flowers will bring extra joy to any room.

14

Old Reliables

sunchokes, egyptian onions, rhubarb & blackcurrants

NONE OF THE perennial vegetables I am growing are particularly versatile. They're also not necessarily my favorite vegetables. So why do I keep them around? What exactly is their claim to fame? In a word—dependability. They are, in fact, so dependable that it didn't seem necessary to dedicate a chapter specifically to growing them.

They sprout up, year after year, with little to no attention and, if all else fails, they will be there in the spring to provide some much needed sustenance at a time when nothing else is even close to ready for harvesting and when everything that was put away from the previous year's harvest is all but gone.

Because perennials keep coming back every year, they tend to outgrow their allotted space and need to be "thinned out" or split, every so often (fall is the best time to do this, but early spring works too). Chances are that someone in the neighborhood will have an unruly patch of rhubarb, or a forest of sunchokes which definitely need thinning. Most gardeners are more than happy to share any excess root stock. Farmers' markets and yard sales are also good places to pick up perennial plants.

Rhubarb sprouts from woody tubers that grow quite close to the surface and can usually be broken apart quite easily. Sunchokes also grow from tubers, but these are fleshy rather than woody, and they're usually several inches deep in the ground. Egyptian onions can be started from a clump off the mother plant but they also grow quickly from bulbils. Even though Egyptian onions are incredible prolific and insanely easy to grow, I did have a bit of difficulty finding some to get my patch started. Now I can't give them away.

Blackcurrant bushes might be a little harder to come by. They can be grown from a handful of berries if you have lots of patience and don't mind waiting a few years for a harvest. I bought my first bushes at an end of season nursery sale and they have served me well, even though I haven't been as diligent as I should have been in pruning them. The berries form on three year old wood, so, on the fourth year and every year after that, any older wood and damaged branches should be removed when the bush is dormant.

Like most plants, perennials like good soil and because they will be rooted in the same spot for several, if not many years, it's important to make sure that the ground is well prepared with the addition of compost and perhaps some very well-rotted manure. I also like to add a sprinkle of blood and bone meal. Future feedings can be applied as top dressings—that is laid on top of the ground circling the plants—but it's important to note that rhubarb especially, even though it's a very greedy plant that loves manure, does not like the manure to touch its roots.

It's best to have a dedicated patch for perennials where they can do their own thing, undisturbed and not interfering with more tender annual crops. Sunchokes will tend to spread rapidly into any open space and it's definitely not a good idea to plant them in a bed that's dedicated to annuals! Egyptian onions are easier to control just as long as their "walking" parts—clumps of bulbils that form on tall stems—are harvested in the fall.

There are other perennial vegetables that are not on my list for the simple reason that I have not been able to grow them here. Asparagus is one of these and a source of much frustration and disappointment because I love asparagus. I believe it likes sandy soil and I'm choosing this as my reason for defeat, although I know one of

my attempts to get a patch established here was foiled by the ducks, who seemed to think that I had spent several hours preparing the bed and planting the delicate green asparagus slips just for them. And they never even said thank you, as they moseyed off along the path leaving an occasional shred of asparagus fern in their wake. Very rude!

Dandelions and stinging nettles are two highly nutritious and totally reliable crops that don't need any encouragement to keep returning, year after year, but as this book is dedicated to easing the way into a closer relationship with everyday food I decided that stinging nettle soup and dandelion greens might be rushing things just a bit, so I left them out.

Much as I'd love to be able to grow Globe (or true) artichokes I haven't even tried because I know they wouldn't stand a chance in our chilly climate. They are a perennial vegetable but they like zone seven plus and warmer. I'm not being defeatist, I'm just being realistic! I know regular artichokes won't survive, but Jerusalem artichokes thrive.

SUNCHOKES

Sunchokes, a.k.a. Jerusalem artichokes, might also, initially, seem like a bit of a weird choice to mention here, especially as they might already be quite familiar, but as flowers rather than as vegetables. A simple shift in perception might be all that's required to make them seem perfectly palatable and the fact that these knobbly little tubers are mentioned in *Larousse Gastronomique* (a well-respected source related to haute cuisine) might be just what's needed to give them a shove in the right direction, into the kitchen that is. Sunchokes/Jerusalem artichokes are bona fide vegetables, that's clear, but exactly what to call them, not so much.

They have gathered up quite a variety names over the years, the two most common in these parts being sunchokes and Jerusalem artichokes. The latter of these two is thought to come from the English mispronunciation of the Italian *girasole articiocco*. The word

◀ Sunchokes—scrubbed clean and ready for roasting.

SUNCHOKE PÂTÉ

Jennifer's Fab Recipe

1 C ground nuts (hazelnuts,
    almonds or walnuts)
2 cloves of garlic
1 C sunchokes (washed but
    not peeled)
2 Tbsp nutritional yeast
2 Tbsp olive oil
2 Tbsp tamari
2 Tbsp lemon juice
1 tsp rosemary

Put all ingredients except rosemary in a food processor and
pulse until smooth. Spread in
oiled ovenproof dish and sprinkle
rosemary on top. Bake at 350°F
for about 55 minutes. Cool before
serving on crackers, in a sandwich, or straight from the spoon!

girasole reflects the fact that the bright yellow flowers turn their faces to follow the sun in its journey across the sky, *gira* meaning turn and *sole* meaning sun. I can never quite decide which name to use, but for the rest of this book I think it will be sunchoke, just because it's a bit more concise.

Sunchokes used to be way more popular than they are today, and it's definitely time they were brought back into favor as a respectable source of excellent nutrition, definitely equal to, if not surpassing, potatoes.

Preparing Sunchokes

The overall shape of a sunchoke tends towards round or cylindrical, typically dotted with several knobbly growth points which make for a lot of waste if the chokes are to be peeled. Fortunately the skin is thin and very smooth, a light tan color with a pleasant pinkish cast (varies somewhat depending on the variety) and really quite attractive. It's definitely better not to peel but simply to scrub the chokes with a fairly stiff brush. They can be sliced thinly and eaten raw or finely chopped and added to dips. They're crisp, crunchy and reminiscent of water chestnuts in texture, with a sweetish, nutty flavor.

Cooking Sunchokes

Even though their texture seems to be quite dense, sunchokes cook up relatively quickly and make a great addition to stir fries. When I'm using them for this purpose I like to cut them into sticks about three times the size of a wooden match. No particular reason why— just personal preference and, in fact, when it comes to slicing chokes it probably makes more sense to slice them crosswise to create medallions that will range in size from a quarter to a silver dollar, and occasionally to a size just short of a canning jar lid.

Sunchokes really don't boil well (does anything) but they're brilliant roasted. It's fairly easy to overcook them so best to keep a close eye on them after twenty minutes or so in a 350°F oven. There seems to be a sweet spot of "doneness" and then it's all downhill, fast. I've found it better to test with a fork rather than by squeezing as I do when baking potatoes. Once the choke feels soft it's probably a bit overdone and the flesh will seem a bit slimy, for want of a better word. The taste will still get a thumbs up but the texture, not so much.

Sunchoke Strata

Larger sized chokes can be sliced lengthwise and used like mini strips of lasagna. One of my "brilliant" inventions is a strata made with layers of sunchoke strips, alternated with sautéed mushrooms and steamed greens, moistened with a little stock—often the liquid that came off the steamed greens, with just a little balsamic or some herbs added—and baked. The gourmet version also includes chopped walnuts or hazelnuts.

One of the best things about "stratas" is their flexibility. For instance I could replace mushrooms with chickpeas, or I could replace them both with onions and feta cheese or whatever else I might have on hand. If I felt like the creamy comfort food version, I might replace the stock with some cream of mushroom soup. Whatever choices I make, this casserole is bound to be tasty and nutritious. And if the chokes are in season, well this pretty much guarantees that the garden will also be bursting with spring salad greens, the perfect accompaniment to a strata.

Harvesting Sunchokes

Unlike most seasonal crops, chokes can be harvested at two separate times, either in the spring or fall. I think it's important to honor their role as a spring crop. The first few months of the year, are also known as "the hungry months," traditionally a time when winter provisions are all but gone and the year's new crops are not even close to being ready for harvesting. In the fall there are so many other foods to choose from that we don't need to eat sunchokes. It's much wiser to save them for a time when we might have nothing else to rely on.

HUNGRY MONTH SOUP
Lightly brown several Egyptian onions and a couple of garlic cloves in some olive oil or butter, then add a couple of pounds of peeled and sliced sunchokes (this can also include a couple of potatoes) along with five cups of stock, and simmer. When the sunchokes are tender a bunch of chopped, early greens such as kale or arugula can be added (if available) and cooked for just a minute or two, until wilted. The soup is then seasoned, blended and served.

▲ The great perennial onion—first up in the spring and still available for harvesting when the snow flies.

Spring is also when perennial onions are at their most welcome so the rather obvious combo is a Sunchoke Onion soup, that I'm calling Hungry Month soup.

EGYPTIAN ONIONS

Perennial onions, like sunchokes, have several names, the most common seeming to be walking or Egyptian onions. The name walking onion obviously comes from this plant's way of "walking" its progeny across the garden, as described in Chapter Five. The origins of the name Egyptian onions are less clear. Interestingly the ancient Egyptians held onions to be very sacred. The concentric circles were thought to symbolize eternal life, to the extent that they have often been discovered in tombs and were even discovered inserted into the eye sockets of Ramesses IV. Enough already? Okay.

Also, the sideways walking pattern of these onions might have been reminiscent of the quintessentially Egyptian hieroglyph: humans walking "sideways." I like to think that the onions in my garden are part of an ancient tradition and therefore I choose to call them Egyptian onions. Besides, walking onions sounds so much more "pedestrian." :)

Cooking with Egyptian Onions

There's not a whole lot to say about how to use these onions that hasn't been said already in Chapter Eleven. Much like any onion they can be included in a host of dishes such as soups, stews, casseroles, quiches, frittatas and so on. They do take a little longer to prepare as they tend to grow in clumps with multiple skins binding them together. I find it best to prepare a bunch and keep them wrapped in damp paper towel in the crisper. They'll keep fresh like this for a week or more.

Personally, I haven't bought into the Paleo diet trend which attempts to simulate/emulate/replicate (?) the diet of our very distant ancestors from the Paleolithic era. For one thing, we don't have many hairy mammoths around these parts any more. However, if I was attempting to eat Paleo I believe that both sunchokes and Egyptian onions would fit in well with my menu plan, in that they are both perennial in the best sense of the word; and because they are totally self-sustaining, it's not hard to imagine that they've been flourishing, virtually unchanged, for a very long time. Certainly Native Americans were cultivating sunchokes long before the arrival of the Europeans and, as already stated, the Egyptians were worshipping onions as sacred in ancient times.

RHUBARB CHUTNEY

Mix together in a large pot:

6 C chopped rhubarb
1 C chopped onion
1 C of raisins
2 C of brown sugar
1½ C of apple cider vinegar
2 tsp finely chopped fresh ginger
3 garlic cloves finely chopped
1 tsp allspice
1 tsp ground ginger
1½ half tsp of cinnamon
½ tsp of ground cloves
1 tsp of salt

Simmer on a low heat until thickened, thirty minutes to an hour, pour into sterile jars and process in a water bath for thirty minutes. This might seem to have a long list of ingredients but it's so simple to make and so delicious, especially with heavier, winter meals, and oh so perfect with curries, that it's more than worth it.

RHUBARB

It's now time to gather up a bag of breadcrumbs, enough to sprinkle a sizeable trail, to ensure finding a way back out of the Rhubarb Forest. Yes, my rhubarb patches are somewhat monumental! Fortunately I have enough friends and neighbors who don't grow rhubarb, but who love to eat it.

Cooking Rhubarb

Rhubarb is totally perennial and also quite seasonal, in that it picks best in the cooler weather, usually through May/June and possibly a little way into July, depending on the weather. The timing is perfect as most of the other fruits and berries are not yet available in the garden. I like rhubarb best simply chopped and simmered or stewed in the tiniest bit of water with some sugar or maple syrup. It makes a lovely breakfast cooked this way and served with yoghurt, topped with a little granola. Replace the yoghurt with ice cream and it becomes a decadent desert. Muffins, pies, crumbles and crisps all lend themselves well to the tangy sweetness of rhubarb.

Another rhubarb staple around here is rhubarb chutney. Generally we're not that fond of condiments and preserves but this is one that we consume in quantity. It seems to go especially well with curries and other spicy rice dishes. It's also delicious spread on a wrap or on a sandwich, or with just about anything else that might lend itself to a sweet fruity chutney. And, it's not at all difficult to make.

BLACKCURRANTS

Blackcurrants are in some ways similar to rhubarb in that they're equally tart, certainly not a pick and eat kind of fruit, and they're easy peasey perennials. They have a very characteristic aroma that I'm not even going to try to describe, except to assure you that it's not in the least unpleasant, simply quite distinctive.

Anyone who grew up in England is probably familiar with Ribena. It is a commercially produced cordial made from blackcurrants,

▲ Simple turned sublime with a topping of blackcurrant pickle.

which is claimed to have an extremely high vitamin C content. Hot Ribena and bed was the go-to cure for colds in my house and this all makes complete sense considering that 100 g of blackcurrants provides 300 times the daily vitamin C requirement.

Another interesting fact I discovered about blackcurrants is that they're said to grow well *where summers are humid and winters are severe and chilling.* That goes a long way to explaining why they do

BLACKCURRANT SWEET PICKLE

4 C blackcurrants

3 C moist brown sugar

1 C seedless raisins

1 C chopped apple

2 Tbsp crushed mustard seeds

2 Tbsp chopped onion

1 Tbsp ground Ginger

1 tsp salt

2 C white vinegar

Cover currants and apple with vinegar, cook gently until tender.

Let cool, then mix in other ingredients. Stir well.

Boil for 10 mins, spoon into sterilized jars, and process in a water bath for fifteen minutes.

BLACKCURRANT COULIS

In the winter, when weekend breakfast might just be buckwheat pancakes, there's nothing quite like a blackcurrant coulis to finish them off. A coulis is really nothing more than fruit simmered in a little water and sugar to taste. Traditionally a coulis is blended into a smooth sauce but I prefer to leave the berries squished but still whole. Blackcurrant coulis on ice cream . . . amazing! Surely the easiest of decadent desserts.

Just another good reason to keep several small (1 cup size) bags of frozen berries in the freezer.

so well here on QuackaDoodle Farm and also in England. They do seem to be much more popular in England than in Canada and of course, in Nova Scotia, if you're not a blueberry you're automatically designated second class in the berry world, even though blackcurrants are much easier to pick and store much better than blueberries, and blueberries don't come close to matching the vitamin and mineral content of blackcurrants.

The downside is that blackcurrants don't eat well straight off the branch because they're sour. They do, however, make the best ever jam which, when paired with cheese (and especially blue cheese) is out of this world. I have heard that vodka or brandy based blackcurrant cordials are very simple to make and are, quite simply, stunning. Recently, I also came across a recipe to make a non-alcoholic cordial, something I'd been searching for—for a while. Color me a deep rich magenta excited!

sirens

Reach up. Into the dank, dust mote gloom
groping along a rustic plank called "shelf"
hand breaking webs of well-fed spiders
searching for the genie jar.
Carry it careful, up creaking stairwell
where, in the bright kitchen,
dust free now it winks a promise
but coyly plays it hard
to get that lid to pop.
It doesn't wait for bread
but jumps onto the tongue
with its purple Summer magic
of sun filtered through branches
burdened,
over burdened with bunches
great bundles of shining berries
exuding their musk
seductive scent luring me
as I crawled, scratched and poked
thinking only of the sweet tang thrill
of black currant jam.

Previously published in *Open Heart Farming*

15

Harvest Time

preserving the garden's gifts

FALL ALWAYS FEELS like such a bittersweet time of year. Summer never seems long enough, even though some of our most beautiful days come in October. Sometimes I wish I could tether the sun, keep it from moving away, just so I could hold onto summer for just a little while longer. These thoughts soon pass, pushed aside by the great new joy this season brings. Harvest time! For several weeks it seems the kitchen is cluttered with bowls and baskets overflowing with fresh picked food, in all shapes, colors and sizes. What a wonderful sight! And also what a feeling: awe, mixed with pride; and doubt, tinged with confusion. What to do with all this food?

FREEZING

Freezing is one way to keep most of the summer freshness around for several months. The important—no, make that essential—step here is blanching. Most, if not all vegetables, should be blanched before freezing. To do so effectively will require a submersible wire basket or, at the very least, a colander. After they have been cleaned and chopped into suitable sizes, the vegetables are plunged into rapidly boiling water, but not for long. Precise blanching times vary slightly depending on the vegetable but are usually around three to four minutes. The intent here is to halt the enzyme action which makes vegetables turn mushy and tasteless even when frozen, but not to cook the vegetables. After appropriate blanching time, the vegetables are removed from the boiling water and immediately plunged into icy cold water to cool them off as quickly as possible. If the pieces are all bundled into a freezer bag prior to freezing, they are likely to freeze as a solid clump. It's much better to spread them as a single layer on a cookie sheet to freeze, and then pack them in freezer bags. Personally, I'm not a great fan of freezing, if it can be avoided, as our power supply is not always reliable, and a power outage that lasts for more than a couple of days can jeopardize a whole freezer full of food.

COLD ROOM STORAGE

Many vegetables such as carrots, potatoes, beets and leeks will store well for several months in a specially designated cold room or root cellar. It's not difficult to set up a cold room in one corner of the basement, if such a space is available. It's a simple matter of insulating to keep the heat out rather than in. Vegetables intended for this type of storage should not be washed. Sun curing—allowing the sun to dry and toughen up the skin slightly—will dry off any excess soil, which can be gently brushed off. It's important to make sure that the skins are thoroughly dry.

I've always stored my potatoes and such between layers of newsprint in plastic laundry hampers. However, the new way of thinking is to limit airflow by layering root crops with wood chips or sawdust in a tall pail or box lined with a plastic garbage bag. The bag is all but closed up, leaving only a softball-sized opening at the top. I have not yet used this method but the very impressive results I've seen have convinced me to give it a try.

It's always a good idea to vary the approach when trying something new, rather than putting all your eggs (or actually, potatoes) into the same basket. With this in mind, I plan to store half this year's crop the "new" way and half using the tried and true method, which I know works reasonably well.

WATER BATH METHOD

WATER BATH METHOD

The water bath method processes pickles and fruits by boiling the canning jars after they have been filled. This method is perfectly reliable just as long as everything is kept sterile. Here's how. After the jars and lids have been washed in hot soapy water, rinsed and drained, the jars are put on a cookie sheet in an oven preheated to 250°F. Twenty minutes is sufficient time to ensure that the jars are sterile. The jar lids, called snap-top lids, will be heated (but not boiled) in a small pan of water.

In the meantime the pickle mixture, let's say it's rhubarb chutney, is bubbling on the stove top according to the specifics of the recipe. When the mix is ready, the jars are removed from the oven and the mix is ladled into the jars.

Before the lids go on it's important to make sure the necks of the jars are clean, enabling the lids to form a tight seal. With the lids in place, the jars are then "processed" in the water bath, which is simply a large pot full of boiling water. It's important to keep the jars covered with at least an inch of water and to keep the water boiling for the recommended amount of time, usually about fifteen minutes. The jars are then removed from the water and left to cool. I always stand them on a cutting board covered with a clean, dry dish towel. Very soon "popping" sounds will indicate that the lids have sealed properly. The pop is made by a small disc in the center of the lid which sucks down as the lid forms a tight seal.

Very occasionally one of the lids doesn't pop down, which indicates that the seal is faulty, leaving the contents of the jar open to contamination over time. Any such jars should therefore be refrigerated and used within a few weeks. The lid popping must never be encouraged by pushing down on the disc manually. This must always be allowed to happen naturally, as a safety measure which indicates that the food will be properly preserved.

Leeks will store best with their roots standing in a bucket of dirt, and of course they are happiest of all left outside until the ground becomes too hard to dig.

PICKLING AND CANNING

Pickling and canning—there is a difference. Pickling uses vinegar/salt as a preservative, whereas canning relies solely on heat, and requires a pressure canner for low acid foods to eliminate any risk of contamination. Fruits, such as peaches and pears, are low in acid but can be safely canned by using the water bath method and replacing the vinegar/salt preservative with sugar syrup.

EQUIPMENT

Technically, pickling can be done without any special equipment other than a pan large enough to be a suitable water bath but, without

▶ A few very simple tools help make preserving summer goodness a snap.

a few simple, inexpensive tools, it can turn into a frustrating and potentially dangerous task. A wire basket for containing a batch of jars and lowering them in and out of the water bath, a plastic funnel especially designed to guide the mixture into the jars while keeping the necks clean, a pair of tongs for lifting the jars in and out of the water bath and a wand with a magnetic tip for lifting the lids from the hot water and placing them on the jars without contaminating them, are all invaluable. Kits containing all these items are readily available, especially just prior to pickling season. However, they tend to be ridiculously over-priced and it's way more economical to purchase the four items mentioned above separately, at a fraction of the price, from a local discount store.

I only use proper canning jars and I never use the lids twice—maybe they will work the second time, maybe they won't, but considering the overall value of the vegetables and my time, I just don't think it's worth the risk.

A CAUTIONARY TALE

As mentioned in the Garden section some varieties of cucumber are specifically for pickling. They tend to be highly prolific, producing lots of smallish, pickle-sized fruit. They need to be picked and processed when they're still small enough to be nice and firm and dark green. Years ago I made dill pickles using regular table salt. I didn't have any "pickling" salt and salt is salt, right? Well, no. Not in this case. The pickles turned cloudy. No one would eat them because they didn't look "right" and I ended up throwing them all away. I was so miffed I didn't make dill pickles for a long time after that!

JAMS AND JELLIES

I usually only make blackcurrant jam so I'm certainly not an expert on this topic, but as far as I can tell the main difference between jam and jelly is that the pulp and seeds are strained out of jelly before it's bottled so that it becomes clear and smooth, whereas the fruit residue is left in jam.

I use artificial pectin when I make jam primarily because it's easier and more reliable, but also because typically it requires a much shorter boiling time as well as less sugar. The more traditional method requires an extensive boiling down of the ingredients (fruit and sugar) and then a wrinkle test on a chilled plate. This is the part I find tedious and frustrating. The method is to drop a dollop of jam on a cold surface and if it wrinkles when moved this means the jam has set. Sounds simple enough except that it might require multiple testings and there's no guarantee that the jam will not be over-boiled (too stiff) when opened, or too runny. In my opinion commercially produced pectin is definitely the way to go, and they supply multiple recipes right in the package.

TIME FOR TEA AND CAKE— GATHERING POPPY SEEDS

From boiling water baths and bubbling mixtures that infuse the kitchen with their spicy aromas I'm going to end with things cool and serene—poppies and chamomile. A typical semi-wild poppy develops a rather unique seed head about the size of a large grape that's perfectly designed to act much like a salt shaker. As the seeds inside are maturing the outer skin is drying and turning from green to brown. Eventually it will turn brittle, split open at the slightest touch, often just from the wind, and scatter hundreds of seeds. Obviously, once the seed head has dried to this degree it's pretty much impossible to gather the seeds so it's important to gather the seed heads shortly after the petals have fallen, when the heads are sun cured and just beginning to dry. This is the time to pick a bunch and hang them upside down in a dry place, encased in a large bag or an old pillow case—the latter is definitely my pick. After a couple of weeks, when the heads are thoroughly dried out, all the seeds will be released into the pillowcase.

The seeds are tiny and collecting them might sound like an arduous task, but no, because they're also very numerous it's really amazing how many can be collected using this simple method.

▲ Poppy seed heads dry quickly releasing hundreds of tiny seeds.

Poppy seeds collected from the garden bring with them memories of glorious petals and brilliant summer days when added to dressings and breads, both sweet and savory, and really, what's nicer than a slice of lemon poppy seed cake? (Please refer to page 18 regarding types of poppy to grow).

CHAMOMILE TEA

If poppies are the yang, with their bold displays of brash color, chamomile definitely provides the yin to create a perfect balance.

Chamomile is a sweet, gentle little plant that develops masses of shiny faced little daisy-type flowers with white petals and yellow centers. Working around them is pleasure enough as their aroma is lovely but also, when dried, they make a wonderful sleepy-time tea. The best way to dry the flowers is in a cool dry place with as much airflow as possible. In other words, simply heaping them in a bowl is certainly not the best way to go. A well perforated colander works better and wire mesh is better still. The mesh (window screening perhaps), stretched over a frame or in the form of a sieve, should be big enough to allow the flowers to be tossed and shuffled every couple of days until they're fully dried. Once dried the tiny flowers make a lovely tea all by themselves or they can be mixed with other herbs or flavors, such as a little dried apple, to create your own perfect tisane blend.

What better way to end a day and, in fact, this book, than to settle back with a cup of chamomile tea and dreams of all the magnificent harvests to come.

About the Author

JENNI BLACKMORE is a farmer, artist, and writer who built her house on a rocky, windswept island off the coast of Nova Scotia almost twenty-five years ago and has been stumbling along the road to self-sufficient living ever since. As a successful micro-farmer she produces most of her family's meat, eggs, fruit, and vegetables, in spite of often-challenging conditions. Jenni is certified as a Permaculture Design Consultant from the Falls Brook Centre in New Brunswick, and is the author of *Permaculture for the Rest of Us*, along with two fiction titles for children and one for adults.

a note about the publisher

New Society Publishers is an activist, solutions-oriented publisher focused on publishing books for a world of change. Our books offer tips, tools, and insights from leading experts in sustainable building, homesteading, climate change, environment, conscientious commerce, renewable energy, and more — positive solutions for troubled times.

We're proud to hold to the highest environmental and social standards of any publisher in North America. This is why some of our books might cost a little more. We think it's worth it!

▶ We print all our books in North America, never overseas

▶ All our books are printed on **100% post-consumer recycled paper**, processed chlorine-free, with low-VOC vegetable-based inks (since 2002)

▶ Our corporate structure is an innovative employee shareholder agreement, so we're one-third employee-owned (since 2015)

▶ We're carbon-neutral (since 2006)

▶ We're certified as a B Corporation (since 2016)

At New Society Publishers, we care deeply about *what* we publish — but also about *how* we do business.

New Society Publishers
ENVIRONMENTAL BENEFITS STATEMENT

For every 5,000 books printed, New Society saves the following resources:[1]

30	Trees
2,695	Pounds of Solid Waste
2,965	Gallons of Water
3,867	Kilowatt Hours of Electricity
4,899	Pounds of Greenhouse Gases
12	Pounds of HAPs, VOCs, and AOX Combined
7	Cubic Yards of Landfill Space

[1]Environmental benefits are calculated based on research done by the Environmental Defense Fund and other members of the Paper Task Force who study the environmental impacts of the paper industry.

Certified B Corporation

FSC MIX Paper from responsible sources FSC® C016245

new society PUBLISHERS
www.newsociety.com